Country Living Recipes

JEAN WICKSTROM LILES

Oxmoor House, Inc.
Birmingham

Cover: *Mexican Cornbread (page 2) is a success with
jalapeño peppers, corn, and cheese added to give
cornbread a new, spicy flavor.*

Page i: *A rich tomato sauce filled with flavorful
ingredients makes Easy Spaghetti Dinner (page 34) a
favorite.*

Page ii: *Yellow squash, zucchini, green pepper, tomato, and onion combine to make a colorful and
tasty Squash Medley (page 84).*

Contents

Author's Note

Year after year Progressive Farmer *continues to provide the South with irresistible recipes and a rich source of entertaining ideas. In an area where people enjoy good old-fashioned home cooking, Southern hospitality has always been a strong tradition. And* Progressive Farmer *has played an important role in strengthening this tradition as Southern homemakers rely on our recipes to please the appetites of family and friends.*

Country Living Recipes *brings together all of the recipes published in* Progressive Farmer *during 1981 plus over one hundred country classic recipes selected from previous issues of the magazine. These come from the best cooks throughout the South who favor us with their family's favorite recipes.*

These recipes are tested, tasted, and reviewed by our staff of experienced home economists prior to publication in Progressive Farmer. *Although taste is a primary consideration in our evaluation, the appearance of a dish adds much to its overall appeal. In view of the active pace of most people's lives and the increased cost of living, ease and cost are also important factors in reviewing our recipes.*

To keep the testing realistic, our home economists test each recipe in kitchens much like yours. They confirm measurement of ingredients, temperature, number of servings—all the specific information that makes Progressive Farmer's *recipes completely reliable.*

In addition to the collection of special Southern recipes, the Pickling and Preserving chapter offers techniques for year-round enjoyment of fruits and vegetables from your garden. The Appendices is an extensive cooking and kitchen guide with charts, tables, and helpful hints for beginners as well as experienced cooks. And the Index cross-indexes recipes by ingredient and by category, making it easy to find any recipe included in the book.

Enjoy your Country Living Recipes. *We believe you'll find this cookbook a welcome and helpful addition to your kitchen library. If you'd like to share with us one of your favorite recipes, do write us. In the meantime, we hope this cookbook will make cooking and eating in your home a little easier and a lot more fun.*

Jean Wickstrom Liles

Breads

WHOLE WHEAT BISCUITS

1 package dry yeast
2 teaspoons warm water (105° to 115°)
2½ cups whole wheat flour
½ cup all-purpose flour
2 teaspoons baking powder
½ teaspoon salt
½ teaspoon soda
¼ cup margarine, softened
1 tablespoon honey
1 cup buttermilk
Melted butter or margarine

Dissolve yeast in warm water; set aside.
Combine dry ingredients; cut in margarine until mixture resembles coarse meal. Add yeast mixture, honey, and buttermilk, mixing well. Turn dough out onto a floured surface. Roll dough to ½-inch thickness; cut into rounds with a 2-inch cutter. Place biscuits on lightly greased baking sheets. Brush with melted butter. Bake at 400° for 12 to 15 minutes. Yield: about 1 dozen.
Mrs. W. P. Chambers,
Louisville, Ky.

RAISED BISCUITS

1 package dry yeast
1 tablespoon sugar
2 tablespoons warm water (105° to 115°)
2 cups self-rising flour
2 tablespoons shortening
⅔ cup buttermilk

Dissolve yeast and sugar in water; set aside. Place flour in a mixing bowl; cut in shortening until mixture resembles coarse meal. Add buttermilk and yeast mixture, mixing until dough forms a ball. With lightly floured hands, shape dough into 1½-inch rolls. Cover and place on a lightly greased baking sheet. Let rise in a warm place (85°), free from drafts, about 1 hour or until doubled in bulk. Bake at 425° for 10 to 12 minutes or until light brown. Yield: 1 dozen.
Sylvia Stephens,
New Hill, N.C.

OLD-FASHIONED BUTTERMILK BISCUITS

4 cups all-purpose flour
2 tablespoons baking powder
1 teaspoon soda
¾ teaspoon salt
1 tablespoon sugar
⅔ cup margarine, softened
1½ cups buttermilk
¼ cup margarine, melted

Combine flour, baking powder, soda, salt, and sugar; cut in ⅔ cup margarine until mixture resembles coarse meal. Add buttermilk, stirring until dry ingredients are moistened. Turn dough out onto a lightly floured surface; knead lightly 4 or 5 times.
Roll dough to ¾-inch thickness; cut with a 2¾-inch biscuit cutter. Place biscuits on a lightly greased baking sheet; brush tops with melted margarine. Bake at 450° for 15 minutes or until golden brown. Yield: 15 biscuits.

MEXICAN CORNBREAD

1 cup self-rising cornmeal
½ teaspoon soda
½ teaspoon salt
½ teaspoon sugar
3 eggs, beaten
1 cup milk
3 jalapeño peppers, seeded and chopped
½ cup chopped onion
1½ cups (6 ounces) shredded Cheddar cheese
1 teaspoon garlic powder
1 (7-ounce) can whole kernel corn, drained
1 (2-ounce) jar chopped pimiento, drained
⅓ cup bacon drippings

Combine cornmeal, soda, salt, and sugar; stir in remaining ingredients. Pour into a greased 10-inch iron skillet. Bake at 350° for 45 minutes or until golden brown. Yield: 12 to 15 servings.

SOUR CREAM CORNBREAD

1 (8½-ounce) can cream-style corn
1 (8-ounce) carton commercial sour cream
2 eggs
½ cup vegetable oil
1 cup self-rising cornmeal
2 teaspoons baking powder

Combine corn, sour cream, eggs, and oil; beat well. Combine cornmeal and baking powder; stir into corn mixture. Pour into a greased 10-inch iron skillet and bake at 400° for 30 minutes or until done. Yield: 8 servings.

Gail Thompson,
Montgomery, Ala.

CORNBREAD PATTIES

3 cups self-rising cornmeal
1 (17-ounce) can cream-style corn
⅔ cup evaporated milk
1 medium onion, chopped
2 eggs, beaten
2 tablespoons bacon drippings
1 tablespoon sugar

Combine all ingredients and stir well. Drop batter by heaping tablespoonfuls into a hot, greased skillet; shape into 3-inch circles with the back of a spoon. Cook until golden, turning once. Yield: about 4 dozen. *Zola Kindred,*
Richmond, Ky.

GOLDEN HUSH PUPPIES

2 cups self-rising cornmeal
1 small onion, finely chopped
¾ cup milk
1 egg, slightly beaten
Vegetable oil

Combine cornmeal and onion; add milk and egg, stirring well. Carefully drop batter by tablespoonfuls into deep hot oil (370°); cook only a few at a time, turning once. Fry until hush puppies are golden brown (3 to 5 minutes). Drain well on paper towels. Yield: about 2 dozen.

SPOONBREAD

1 cup cornmeal
3 cups milk, divided
1 teaspoon salt
1 teaspoon baking powder
2 tablespoons vegetable oil
3 eggs, separated
Butter or margarine

Combine cornmeal and 2 cups milk, stirring until blended. Cook over low heat until the consistency of mush. Remove from heat; add salt, baking powder, oil, and remaining 1 cup milk. Beat egg yolks. Gradually stir about one-fourth of hot mixture into yolks, stirring well; stir yolk mixture into hot mixture. Beat egg whites (at room temperature) until stiff peaks form; fold into cornmeal mixture. Spoon into a greased 2-quart casserole. Bake at 325° for 1 hour. Serve spoonbread hot with butter. Yield: about 6 servings. *Debra Lancaster,*
Hawkinsville, Ga.

BANANA MUFFINS

1 cup all-purpose flour
¼ cup sugar
2½ teaspoons baking powder
½ teaspoon soda
½ teaspoon salt
½ teaspoon ground cinnamon
¼ teaspoon ground nutmeg
1 cup mashed banana
½ cup quick-cooking oats, uncooked
½ cup milk
¼ cup butter or margarine, melted
1 egg, beaten

Combine first 7 ingredients, blending thoroughly; make a well in center of mixture. Combine remaining ingredients, stirring well; add to dry ingredients, stirring just until moistened. Fill greased and floured muffin pans two-thirds full. Bake at 425° for 15 minutes or until done. Yield: 1 dozen.

Elizabeth V. Johnson,
Stafford, Va.

FIG MUFFINS

½ cup butter or margarine, softened
1 cup sugar
2 eggs
1½ cups all-purpose flour
2 teaspoons baking powder
½ teaspoon ground cinnamon
¼ teaspoon ground cloves
¼ teaspoon ground allspice
½ cup milk
½ cup fig preserves
½ cup chopped pecans

Cream butter and sugar until light and fluffy; add eggs one at a time, beating well after each addition.

Combine flour, baking powder, and spices; add to creamed mixture alternately with milk, stirring lightly. Add preserves and pecans; stir to blend well. Fill greased and floured muffin pans two-thirds full. Bake at 350° for 15 minutes. Yield: 1 dozen. *Mrs. William R. Boies,*
Mangham, La.

BLUEBERRY MUFFINS

1½ cups all-purpose flour
½ cup sugar
2 teaspoons baking powder
½ teaspoon salt
1 egg
½ cup milk
¼ cup vegetable oil
1 cup fresh blueberries

Combine dry ingredients in a mixing bowl; make a well in center of mixture. Combine egg, milk, and oil; add to dry ingredients, and stir just until moistened. Fold in blueberries. Fill greased muffin pans two-thirds full. Bake at 400° for 20 to 25 minutes. Yield: 1 dozen.

Note: ¾ cup of frozen blueberries, thawed, may be substituted for 1 cup fresh.

Linda K. Smith,
Harrisonburg, Va.

WHEAT GERM-PRUNE MUFFINS

1 egg
¾ cup milk
¼ cup vegetable oil
1 cup all-purpose flour
¾ cup regular wheat germ
¼ cup sugar
2 teaspoons baking powder
½ teaspoon salt
1 cup chopped prunes

Combine egg, milk, and oil in a medium bowl; beat with electric mixer on medium speed until well blended.

Combine dry ingredients; stir into liquid mixture just to moisten. Stir in prunes. Fill greased muffin pans three-fourths full. Bake at 400° for 20 minutes or until muffins test done. Yield: about 9 muffins. *Charlene Stroud,*
Laurens, S.C.

EVER-READY BRAN MUFFINS

1 (15-ounce) package wheat bran flakes cereal
   with raisins
5 cups all-purpose flour
3 cups sugar
1 tablespoon plus 2 teaspoons soda
2 teaspoons salt
4 eggs, beaten
4 cups buttermilk
1 cup vegetable oil

Combine first 5 ingredients in a large bowl; make a well in center of mixture. Add eggs, buttermilk, and oil; stir just enough to moisten dry ingredients. Cover and store in refrigerator until ready to bake. (Batter can be stored in refrigerator up to 6 weeks.)

When ready to bake, fill greased muffin pans two-thirds full. Bake at 400° for 12 to 15 minutes. Yield: about 5½ dozen.

Margaret M. Lewis,
Bowling Green, Va.

FLUFFY SOUR CREAM PANCAKES

3 eggs, separated
1½ cups commercial sour cream
1 teaspoon soda
1¼ cups all-purpose flour
2 teaspoons sugar
1 teaspoon baking powder
½ teaspoon salt
3 tablespoons butter or margarine, softened

Beat egg yolks well. Combine sour cream and soda; stir into egg yolks. Combine flour, sugar, baking powder, and salt; stir into sour cream mixture. Add butter, and beat on medium speed of electric mixer 30 seconds. Beat egg whites (at room temperature) until stiff peaks form; fold whites into batter.

For each pancake, pour about ¼ cup batter onto a hot, lightly greased griddle. Turn pancakes when tops are covered with bubbles and edges look cooked. Yield: 4 to 5 servings.

BUTTERMILK GRIDDLE CAKES

2 cups all-purpose flour
3 tablespoons sugar
2 teaspoons baking powder
1 teaspoon salt
½ teaspoon soda
1 egg, beaten
1½ cups buttermilk
3 tablespoons shortening, melted
Maple Syrup (recipe follows)

Combine dry ingredients. Combine egg and buttermilk; slowly stir into dry ingredients. Add shortening, mixing lightly. Drop mixture by heaping tablespoonfuls onto a hot, lightly greased griddle. Turn pancakes when tops are covered with bubbles and edges look cooked. Serve hot with maple syrup. Yield: 4 to 6 servings.

MAPLE SYRUP:

2 cups water
4 cups sugar
2 teaspoons imitation maple flavoring

Heat water to boiling in a medium saucepan; add sugar and reduce heat. Stir until sugar is dissolved (do not let mixture boil). Remove from heat and add maple flavoring. Serve warm. Store in refrigerator. Yield: 4 cups.

Ansel L. Todd,
Royston, Ga.

SUNDAY MORNING COFFEE CAKE

¼ cup shortening
1 cup sugar
2 eggs, separated
1 teaspoon vanilla extract
1½ cups all-purpose flour
2 teaspoons baking powder
½ teaspoon salt
½ cup milk
Topping (recipe follows)

Cream shortening and sugar until fluffy; add egg yolks and vanilla, mixing well. Combine flour, baking powder, and salt; add to creamed mixture alternately with milk, mixing well after each addition. Beat egg whites (at room temperature) until stiff; fold into batter. Pour into a greased 8-inch square baking pan; sprinkle topping over batter. Bake at 375° for 30 minutes. Yield: one 8-inch coffee cake.

TOPPING:

1 cup sifted powdered sugar
1 tablespoon ground cinnamon
3 tablespoons butter or margarine, softened

Combine all ingredients and mix until crumbly. Yield: about ¾ cup.

Mrs. Paul Raper,
Burgaw, N.C.

Pour batter into a greased and floured 9- x 5- x 3-inch loafpan. Combine 1½ tablespoons sugar and cinnamon; sprinkle evenly over batter. Bake at 350° for 1 hour. Yield: 1 loaf.

Mrs. Stan Unruh,
Sedan, N. Mex.

FRESH APPLE BREAD

1 cup sugar
½ cup shortening
2 eggs
2 cups all-purpose flour
1 teaspoon soda
½ teaspoon salt
1½ tablespoons buttermilk
½ teaspoon vanilla extract
1 cup chopped pecans
1 tablespoon all-purpose flour
1 cup peeled and grated apple
1½ tablespoons sugar
½ teaspoon ground cinnamon

Combine 1 cup sugar and shortening; cream until light and fluffy. Add eggs, one at a time, beating well after each addition.

Combine 2 cups flour, soda, and salt; combine buttermilk and vanilla. Add dry ingredients to creamed mixture alternately with buttermilk mixture, beating well after each addition.

Combine pecans and 1 tablespoon flour; stir well. Stir pecans and apple into batter.

APRICOT-NUT BREAD

1 cup all-purpose flour
¾ cup whole wheat flour
2 teaspoons baking powder
½ teaspoon soda
½ teaspoon salt
½ cup butter or margarine, softened
¾ cup sugar
2 eggs
1 cup mashed banana
¼ cup milk
¾ cup chopped dried apricots
½ cup coarsely chopped pecans

Combine first 5 ingredients; set aside.
Cream butter; gradually add sugar, beating until light and fluffy. Add eggs, one at a time, beating well after each addition.

Combine banana and milk; add to creamed mixture alternately with dry ingredients. Fold in apricots and pecans. Pour batter into a greased and floured 8½- x 4½- x 3-inch loafpan. Bake at 350° for 1 hour or until bread tests done. Yield: 1 loaf.

Lucille Hall,
Bakersfield, Mo.

PUMPKIN-NUT BREAD

3⅓ cups all-purpose flour
½ teaspoon baking powder
2 teaspoons soda
1½ teaspoons salt
1 teaspoon ground cinnamon
1 teaspoon ground cloves
⅔ cup shortening
2 cups sugar
4 eggs
1 (16-ounce) can pumpkin
⅔ cup water
⅔ cup prepared mincemeat
⅔ cup chopped pecans

Combine first 6 ingredients; set aside. Cream shortening and sugar until light and fluffy. Add eggs, one at a time, beating well after each addition. Add pumpkin and mix well. Add dry ingredients to creamed mixture alternately with water; mix well. Add mincemeat and pecans. Spoon into two greased and floured 9- x 5- x 3-inch loafpans; bake at 300° for 1½ hours. Yield: 2 loaves.   *Mrs. Richard Herrington,*
Hermitage, Tenn.

DATE NUT LOAF

2 cups chopped pitted dates
1 teaspoon soda
1 cup boiling water
1 cup firmly packed brown sugar
2 tablespoons shortening
¼ teaspoon salt
1 egg
½ cup chopped pecans
1½ cups all-purpose flour

Place dates in a small bowl; sprinkle soda over dates. Add boiling water and set aside. Cream brown sugar and shortening in a large bowl. Add salt and egg; beat well. Add pecans and date mixture; mix well. Stir in flour. Spoon into a 9- x 5- x 3-inch loafpan. Bake at 325° for 1 hour or until done. Yield: 1 loaf.
Mrs. James T. Orrell,
Hot Springs, Ark.

FROSTED CINNAMON REFRIGERATOR ROLLS

2 packages dry yeast
½ cup warm water (105° to 115°)
2 cups warm milk (105° to 115°)
⅓ cup sugar
1 tablespoon baking powder
2 teaspoons salt
⅓ cup vegetable oil
1 egg
About 7¼ cups all-purpose flour
½ cup sugar
1 tablespoon plus 1 teaspoon ground
    cinnamon
¼ cup butter or margarine, softened
2 cups sifted powdered sugar
3 tablespoons milk
1 teaspoon vanilla extract

Dissolve yeast in warm water; let stand 5 minutes.

Combine 2 cups milk, ⅓ cup sugar, baking powder, and salt in a large mixing bowl; stir well. Add yeast mixture, oil, and egg; stir well. Add 3 cups flour and beat well. Add remaining flour, beating until mixture is smooth and leaves sides of bowl (dough will be sticky).

Turn dough out onto a floured surface; knead until smooth and elastic (about 5 to 8 minutes). Place in a well-greased bowl, turning to grease top. Cover and let rise in a warm place (85°), free from drafts, about 1 hour or until doubled in bulk.

Combine ½ cup sugar and cinnamon; set aside.

Punch dough down and divide in half. Roll each half into a 12- x 10-inch rectangle; spread each with 2 tablespoons butter. Sprinkle each with half of sugar mixture.

Roll up rectangles jellyroll fashion, beginning at longest sides. Pinch edges and ends to seal. Cut each roll into 1-inch slices. Place rolls 1 inch apart on lightly greased baking sheets.

To bake immediately, cover and let rise in a warm place (85°), free from drafts, about 40 minutes or until doubled in bulk. Bake at 350° for 25 to 30 minutes.

Combine powdered sugar, 3 tablespoons milk, and vanilla; spread over hot rolls. Yield: about 2 dozen.

Note: To refrigerate rolls before baking, cover with foil; chill at least 12 hours but no longer than 48 hours. (Liquid may form in pan; do not drain.) To bake, remove foil and bake at 350° for 30 to 35 minutes or until lightly browned. Frost while rolls are hot.

Nina Ward,
Caldwell, Kans.

MORAVIAN SUGAR CAKE

1 package dry yeast
½ teaspoon sugar
¼ cup warm water (105° to 115°)
1 cup unsalted hot mashed potatoes
1 cup sugar
½ cup shortening
¼ cup butter
1 teaspoon salt
2 eggs, beaten
5 to 6 cups all-purpose flour
1 cup cold butter, cut into ⅛-inch slices
1½ cups firmly packed brown sugar
Ground cinnamon

Dissolve yeast and ½ teaspoon sugar in warm water; let stand 5 minutes.

Combine potatoes, 1 cup sugar, shortening, ¼ cup butter, and salt in a large mixing bowl; mix until shortening and butter melt. Stir in yeast mixture. Cover and let rise in a warm place (85°), free from drafts, about 1½ hours or until spongy.

Stir in eggs and enough flour to make a soft dough that leaves sides of bowl. Shape dough into a ball; place in a well-greased bowl, turning to grease top. Cover and let rise in a warm place (85°), free from drafts, about 2 hours or until doubled in bulk.

Turn dough out onto a lightly floured surface, and knead 5 minutes or until smooth and elastic. Divide dough in half; pat evenly into two greased 13- x 9- x 2-inch baking pans. Cover

and let rise in a warm place (85°), free from drafts, about 1½ hours or until doubled in bulk.

Press slices of butter into dough at about ½-inch intervals in rows. Top each slice of butter with about 1 teaspoon brown sugar. Sprinkle cinnamon over entire surface. Bake at 375° for 20 minutes or until golden brown. Cut into 2-inch squares and serve warm. Yield: 42 servings.

Note: Cake may be frozen; remove from freezer and heat at 350° until warm.

Jane C. Webb,
Norris, Tenn.

ORANGE COFFEE CAKE

1 cup water
½ cup shortening
2½ cups all-purpose flour
1 cup corn flakes, crushed
1 package dry yeast
½ cup sugar
1 teaspoon salt
Grated rind of 1 orange
1 egg, beaten
½ teaspoon lemon extract
½ cup firmly packed light brown sugar
2 tablespoons orange juice

Combine water and shortening in a small saucepan; heat until warm (120° to 130°), stirring to melt shortening.

Combine next 6 ingredients in a large bowl; add water mixture. Using low speed of electric mixer, blend until dough is smooth. Add egg and lemon extract; beat until blended.

Spread dough evenly into a greased 9-inch square pan. Cover and let rise in a warm place (85°), free from drafts, about 1 hour or until doubled in bulk.

Bake at 375° for 30 to 35 minutes or until browned. Combine brown sugar and orange juice; stir well. Spoon sugar mixture over hot coffee cake. Cool on a wire rack. Yield: one 9-inch coffee cake. *Mrs. William S. Bell,*
Chattanooga, Tenn.

RAISIN ENGLISH MUFFINS

1 package dry yeast
1 cup warm water (105° to 115°)
1 cup milk
2 tablespoons sugar
1 teaspoon salt
3 tablespoons butter or margarine
1 cup raisins
5½ to 6 cups all-purpose flour
Cornmeal

Dissolve yeast in warm water in a large mixing bowl; let stand 5 minutes.

Combine milk, sugar, salt, and butter in a small saucepan. Cook over medium-low heat, stirring until butter melts. Cool to lukewarm (105° to 115°).

Stir milk mixture, raisins, and 3 cups flour into yeast mixture; beat until smooth. Add remaining flour to form a stiff dough.

Turn dough out onto a floured surface, and knead 2 minutes or until dough can be shaped into a ball (dough will be slightly sticky). Place in a well-greased bowl, turning to grease top. Cover and let rise in a warm place (85°), free from drafts, about 1 hour or until doubled in bulk.

Punch dough down, and divide in half. Turn one half out onto a smooth surface heavily sprinkled with cornmeal. Pat dough into a circle, ½ inch thick, using palms of hands. Cut dough into rounds with a 2¾-inch cutter. (Be sure to cut rounds carefully as leftover dough should not be reused.)

Sprinkle two baking sheets with cornmeal. Transfer cut dough rounds to baking sheets, placing 2 inches apart with cornmeal side down (one side of dough should remain free of cornmeal). Repeat process with remaining half of dough. Cover and let rise in a warm place (85°), free from drafts, about 30 minutes or until doubled in bulk.

Using a wide spatula, transfer rounds to a lightly greased electric skillet preheated to 360°. Place cornmeal side down and cook 6 minutes. Turn muffins and cook an additional 6 minutes. Cool on wire racks. To serve, split muffins and toast until lightly browned. Muffins should be stored in an airtight container. Yield: about 1½ dozen.

Note: Muffins may be cooked over direct medium-high heat in a skillet.

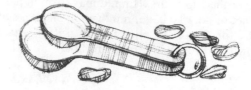

SPICED YEAST DOUGHNUTS

1 package dry yeast
¼ cup warm water (105° to 115°)
¾ cup milk
¼ cup sugar or honey
¾ teaspoon salt
¼ cup butter or margarine
½ teaspoon ground cinnamon
½ teaspoon ground nutmeg
4 cups all-purpose flour, divided
1 egg, beaten
Vegetable oil
Sifted powdered sugar

Dissolve yeast in warm water in a large mixing bowl; let stand 5 minutes.

Combine milk, sugar, salt, butter, and spices in a small saucepan. Cook over medium-low heat, stirring until butter melts. Cool to lukewarm (105° to 115°). Stir milk mixture and 2 cups flour into yeast mixture; beat until smooth. Add egg and remaining flour, mixing to form a soft dough.

Turn dough out onto a floured surface, and knead 5 to 8 minutes or until smooth and elastic. Place in a well-greased bowl, turning to grease top. Cover and let rise in a warm place (85°), free from drafts, about 1 hour or until doubled in bulk.

Punch dough down; let rest 10 minutes. Place dough on a lightly floured surface; roll to ½-inch thickness. Cut with a floured 2½-inch doughnut cutter.

Place doughnuts several inches apart on greased baking sheets; cover and let rise in a warm place (85°), free from drafts, 20 to 25 minutes or until doubled in bulk.

Heat 2 inches of oil to 375°; cook 3 to 4 doughnuts at a time. Cook about 1 minute or until golden on one side; turn and cook other side about 1 minute. Drain on paper towels. Sprinkle with powdered sugar. Yield: about 1½ dozen.   *Kassie Baumann,*
Seminole, Okla.

BUBBLE BREAD

1 cup milk, scalded
½ cup shortening
1½ cups sugar, divided
1 teaspoon salt
1 package dry yeast
2 eggs, beaten
About 3½ cups all-purpose flour
2 teaspoons ground cinnamon
1 cup raisins
1 cup finely chopped pecans
½ cup margarine, melted

Combine milk, shortening, ½ cup sugar, and salt; cool to lukewarm (105° to 115°). Add yeast and stir to dissolve. Stir in eggs. Add flour, mixing well. Turn dough out onto a floured surface, and knead 10 minutes or until smooth and elastic. Place dough in a greased bowl, turning to grease top. Cover and let rise in a warm place (85°), free from drafts, about 1½ hours or until doubled in bulk.

Combine remaining sugar, cinnamon, raisins, and pecans; set aside.

Punch down dough and roll with hands into 1½-inch rolls; dip in margarine and roll in sugar mixture. Place rolls in staggered rows and layers in a well-greased, one-piece 10-inch tube pan. Sprinkle remaining sugar mixture between rolls while arranging, and pour remaining margarine over top. Let rise in a warm place (85°), free from drafts, about 1 hour or until doubled in bulk. Bake at 350° for 45 to 50 minutes. Invert coffee cake on a serving platter. Yield: one 10-inch coffee cake.   *Mrs. W. P. Chambers,*
Louisville, Ky.

NEW ORLEANS FRENCH BREAD

2 tablespoons shortening
1 tablespoon sugar
1 tablespoon salt
1 cup boiling water
1 cup cold water
1 package dry yeast
5½ to 6 cups all-purpose flour
Egg White Glaze (recipe follows)

Combine shortening, sugar, salt, and boiling water in a large bowl, stirring occasionally to melt shortening. Add cold water; cool mixture to lukewarm (105° to 115°). Sprinkle yeast over mixture; let stand 5 minutes, stirring to dissolve.

Gradually beat in 4 cups flour; add enough of the remaining flour to form a stiff dough.

Turn dough out onto a floured surface, and knead until smooth and elastic, about 5 minutes. Place in a well-greased bowl, turning to grease top. Cover and let rise in a warm place (85°), free from drafts, 1 to 1½ hours or until doubled in bulk. Punch dough down. Cover and let rise in a warm place for 30 minutes or until doubled in bulk.

Turn dough out onto a floured surface; knead slightly to press out bubbles. Shape into a 14- to 16-inch cylinder on a large greased baking sheet. Cover and let rise in a warm place (85°), free from drafts, until doubled in bulk.

Cut ¼-inch deep slashes in top of dough with a sharp knife; brush with egg white glaze. Bake at 375° for 40 to 50 minutes or until golden brown. Remove from baking sheet; cool on wire rack. Yield: 1 loaf.

EGG WHITE GLAZE:

1 egg white
2 tablespoons cold water

Combine egg white and water, beating until frothy. Yield: about ¼ cup.

Tip: To thaw frozen bread or rolls, wrap in aluminum foil and heat at 325° for 5 minutes.

RYE AND WHITE BREAD

Rye Dough:

2 packages dry yeast
⅔ cup warm water (105° to 115°)
3 tablespoons molasses
1 tablespoon butter or margarine, melted
2 teaspoons caraway seeds
1 teaspoon salt
About 1½ cups all-purpose flour
1 cup rye flour

Dissolve yeast in warm water in a large bowl; set mixture aside 5 minutes. Stir in molasses, butter, caraway seeds, salt, and flour; mix well.

Turn dough out onto a floured surface, and knead about 5 minutes or until smooth and elastic. Place dough in a greased bowl, turning to grease top. Cover and let rise in a warm place (85°), free from drafts, about 1½ hours or until doubled in bulk.

White Dough:

¼ cup milk, scalded
2 tablespoons sugar
1 teaspoon salt
2 tablespoons butter or margarine, melted
1 package dry yeast
¼ cup warm water (105° to 115°)
1 egg, beaten
1 teaspoon caraway seeds
About 2¼ cups all-purpose flour

Combine milk, sugar, salt, and butter in a small bowl, stirring well; allow to cool to lukewarm (105° to 115°).

Dissolve yeast in warm water in a large bowl; set aside 5 minutes. Stir milk mixture, egg, caraway seeds, and 1 cup flour into yeast mixture; beat until smooth. Stir in remaining 1¼ cups flour to form a soft dough.

Turn dough out onto a floured surface, and knead about 5 minutes or until smooth and elastic. Place dough in a greased bowl, turning to grease top. Cover and let rise in a warm place (85°), free from drafts, about 1 hour or until doubled in bulk.

Shaping the Loaf:

Punch rye dough down; turn out onto a floured surface, and shape into a 14-inch rope. Repeat punching and shaping process with white dough. Place ropes side by side, and firmly pinch ends to seal. Carefully twist ropes together 3 or 4 times; firmly pinch loose ends to seal. Place dough in a greased 9- x 5- x 3-inch loafpan.

Cover and let rise in a warm place (85°), free from drafts, about 45 minutes or until doubled in bulk. Bake at 375° for 30 to 40 minutes or until loaf sounds hollow when tapped. Yield: 1 loaf.

Note: Prepare dough in order given since rye dough will rise more slowly than white dough.
Mrs. Willie S. Carter,
King William, Va.

COTTAGE CHEESE-DILL BREAD

2 packages dry yeast
½ cup warm water (105° to 115°)
2 tablespoons plus 2 teaspoons sugar, divided
2 cups cream-style cottage cheese
2 tablespoons finely chopped onion
2 tablespoons dried dillweed
1 teaspoon baking powder
1 teaspoon salt
2 eggs, beaten
4½ cups all-purpose flour
Melted butter

Dissolve yeast in warm water in a large bowl; stir in 2 teaspoons sugar. Set aside. Combine next 6 ingredients and remaining sugar in a small mixing bowl; add to yeast mixture, mixing well. Gradually add flour, stirring well.

Turn dough out onto a floured surface; knead until smooth and elastic, about 8 to 10 minutes (dough will be sticky). Place in a well-greased bowl, turning to grease top. Cover and let rise in a warm place (85°), free from drafts, about 1 hour or until doubled in bulk.

Punch dough down, and divide in half. Shape each half into a loaf. Place dough in 2 well-greased 8½- x 4½- x 3-inch loafpans. Cover and let rise in a warm place (85°), free from drafts, about 40 minutes or until doubled in bulk. Bake at 350° for 30 to 35 minutes or until loaves sound hollow when tapped. Remove from pans and brush with melted butter. Yield: 2 loaves.   *Rachel V. Youree, Murfreesboro, Tenn.*

NO-KNEAD REFRIGERATOR BREAD

1 package dry yeast
1½ cups warm water (105° to 115°)
⅔ cup sugar
⅔ cup shortening
2 eggs
1 cup warm mashed potatoes
1½ teaspoons salt
About 7½ cups all-purpose flour

Dissolve yeast in warm water in a large mixing bowl. Add sugar, shortening, eggs, potatoes, salt, and 4 cups flour. Beat 30 seconds at low speed of electric mixer; scrape bowl constantly. Beat 2 minutes at medium speed, scraping bowl occasionally. Stir in remaining flour, mixing thoroughly. Place dough in a well-greased bowl, turning to grease top. Cover tightly and refrigerate at least 8 hours or up to 3 days before shaping.

Divide dough in half; shape each half into a loaf. Place in 2 greased 9- x 5- x 3-inch loafpans. Cover and let rise in a warm place (85°), free from drafts, about 3 hours or until doubled in bulk. Bake at 400° for 15 to 20 minutes or until loaves sound hollow when tapped. Yield: 2 loaves.

Note: To make rolls, shape as desired. Place in greased pans. Cover and let rise in a warm place (85°), free from drafts, about 1 hour or until doubled in bulk. Bake at 400° for 10 to 15 minutes. Yield: about 2 dozen.
                    Mrs. Max E. Ayer, Elizabethton, Tenn.

QUICK BUTTERMILK ROLLS

4 to 4½ cups all-purpose flour, divided
2 packages dry yeast
3 tablespoons sugar
1 teaspoon salt
½ teaspoon soda
1¼ cups buttermilk
½ cup water
½ cup shortening

Combine 1½ cups flour, yeast, sugar, salt, and soda in a large bowl, mixing well. Combine buttermilk, water, and shortening in a small saucepan; place over low heat until warm (120° to 130°). Gradually add milk mixture to dry ingredients, mixing at low speed of electric mixer; beat 3 minutes on medium speed. Stir in remaining flour.

Turn dough out onto a lightly floured surface, and knead until smooth and elastic (about 5 minutes). Place dough in a greased bowl, turning to grease top. Cover and let rise in a warm place (85°), free from drafts, about 45 minutes or until doubled in bulk.

Punch dough down and shape into 1½-inch balls; place on a greased 15- x 10- x 1-inch jellyroll pan. Let rise in a warm place (85°), free from drafts, about 35 minutes or until doubled in bulk. Bake at 400° for 18 to 20 minutes. Yield: 2 dozen.   *Mrs. Robert D. Burgess, Fort Smith, Ark.*

BUTTERMILK REFRIGERATOR ROLLS

1 package dry yeast
½ cup warm water (105° to 115°)
½ cup shortening, melted
4½ cups all-purpose flour
¼ cup sugar
1 tablespoon plus 1 teaspoon baking powder
1 teaspoon salt
½ teaspoon soda
2 cups buttermilk

Dissolve yeast in warm water in a large mixing bowl; let stand 5 minutes. Stir in shortening. Combine dry ingredients in a small bowl. Add dry ingredients and buttermilk to yeast mixture; mix well. Turn dough out onto a well-floured surface; knead gently until dough can be handled. Shape into a ball; place in a greased bowl, turning to grease top. Cover and refrigerate until needed. (Dough will keep up to 1 week.)

Shape dough into rolls, as desired; place on lightly greased baking sheets. Bake at 400° for 8 to 10 minutes or until lightly browned. Yield: about 2 dozen.   *Mrs. Larry Doskocil,*
Lott, Tex.

BUTTER-RICH CRESCENT ROLLS

¾ cup milk
1 package dry yeast
¼ cup warm water (105° to 115°)
¼ cup sugar
1 teaspoon salt
¼ cup butter or margarine, softened
1 egg, beaten
3 cups all-purpose flour

Scald milk, and let cool to lukewarm (105° to 115°). Dissolve yeast in warm water in a large bowl. Stir in sugar, salt, butter, and egg. Add milk, stirring well. Add flour and beat until smooth. Place dough in a greased bowl, turning to grease top. Cover and let rise in a warm place (85°), free from drafts, about 1 hour or until doubled in bulk.

Punch dough down, and divide in half. Roll each half into a circle about 10 inches in diameter and ¼ inch thick; cut into 8 wedges. Roll each wedge tightly, beginning at wide end.

Place rolls on greased baking sheets, point side down. Curve into crescent shapes. Cover and let rise in a warm place (85°), free from drafts, about 45 minutes or until doubled in bulk. Bake at 400° for 8 to 10 minutes or until lightly browned. Yield: 16 rolls.

Mrs. Hurley M. Barker,
Milton, N.C.

YEAST BREAD SQUARES

1 package dry yeast
1¼ cups warm water (105° to 115°)
¼ cup shortening
2 tablespoons sugar
1 teaspoon salt
2⅔ cups all-purpose flour
1 tablespoon poppy seeds
Melted butter

Combine yeast and warm water in a large bowl. Add shortening, sugar, salt, and 2 cups flour. Beat 3 minutes at low speed of electric mixer, scraping bowl occasionally. Stir in remaining flour. Cover and let rise in a warm place (85°), free from drafts, about 30 minutes or until doubled in bulk.

Stir dough and spread evenly into a well-greased 13- x 9- x 2-inch baking pan. Sprinkle poppy seeds over top; cover and let rise in a warm place (85°), free from drafts, about 40 minutes or until doubled in bulk. Bake at 375° for 25 to 30 minutes or until golden brown. Brush with melted butter. Cut into 24 squares. Yield: 2 dozen.   *Mrs. Ray Harp,*
Shawnee, Okla.

Bake the fresh flavor of fruit into Apricot-Nut Bread (page 5), Pumpkin-Nut Bread (page 6), Blueberry Muffins (page 3), and Banana Muffins (page 3).

Overleaf: Create an old-fashioned flavor in your kitchen with Ginger Crinkles (page 21).

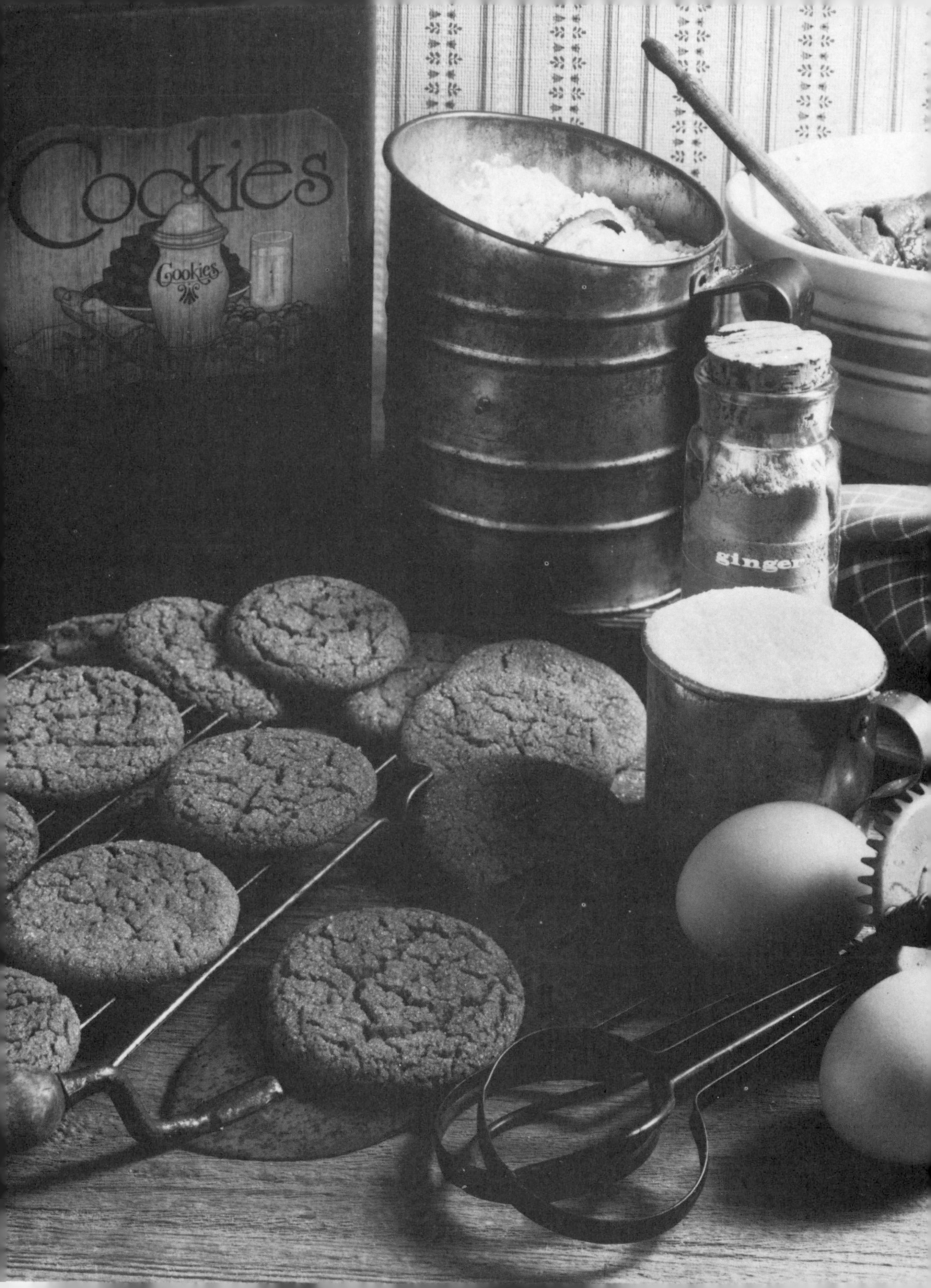
Cookies
Cookies
ginger

Desserts

BEST EVER CHOCOLATE CAKE

½ cup shortening
2 cups sugar
2 eggs
4 (1-ounce) squares unsweetened chocolate, melted
2 cups sifted cake flour
½ teaspoon baking powder
1 teaspoon soda
1 teaspoon salt
¾ cup buttermilk
¾ cup water
1 teaspoon vanilla extract
Chocolate Filling (recipe follows)
Chocolate Frosting (recipe follows)

Cream shortening; gradually add sugar, beating well. Add eggs, one at a time, beating well after each addition. Add melted chocolate, mixing well.

Combine flour, baking powder, soda, and salt; gradually add to chocolate mixture alternately with buttermilk, beating well after each addition. Add water, mixing well; stir in vanilla.

Line the bottoms of two greased 9-inch round cakepans with waxed paper. Pour batter evenly into pans; bake at 350° for 30 minutes or until a wooden pick inserted in center comes out clean. Let cool in pans 10 minutes; remove from pans, and place on wire racks to cool.

Spread chocolate filling between layers. Frost top and sides of cake with chocolate frosting. Yield: one 2-layer cake.

CHOCOLATE FILLING:

2 tablespoons cornstarch
½ cup sugar
Dash of salt
½ cup water
1 tablespoon butter or margarine
2 (1-ounce) squares semisweet chocolate

Combine cornstarch, sugar, salt, and water in a small saucepan; cook over medium heat, stirring constantly, until thickened. Remove from heat and add remaining ingredients, stirring until butter and chocolate are melted. Let cool. Yield: enough for one 2-layer cake.

CHOCOLATE FROSTING:

2 cups sugar
1 cup evaporated milk
½ cup butter or margarine
1 (6-ounce) package semisweet chocolate morsels
1 cup marshmallow creme
2 tablespoons milk
1 tablespoon light corn syrup

Combine sugar, milk, and butter in a medium saucepan; cook over medium heat, stirring constantly, until mixture reaches soft ball stage (234°). Remove from heat; add remaining ingredients, stirring until smooth and chocolate is melted. Let cool slightly; beat until of spreading consistency. Yield: enough for one 2-layer cake.
Shirley Fifer,
Havelock, N.C.

15

GERMAN CHOCOLATE CAKE

1 (4-ounce) package sweet baking chocolate
½ cup water
1 teaspoon vanilla extract
1 cup shortening
2 cups sugar
4 eggs, separated
2½ cups sifted cake flour
1 teaspoon soda
Pinch of salt
1 cup buttermilk
Coconut-Pecan Frosting
Pecan halves (optional)

Combine chocolate and water; bring to a boil, and stir until chocolate melts. Cool; stir in vanilla, and set aside.

Cream shortening; gradually add sugar, beating until light and fluffy. Add egg yolks, one at a time, beating well after each addition. Add chocolate mixture; beat until blended.

Combine flour, soda, and salt; add to creamed mixture alternately with buttermilk, beginning and ending with flour mixture. Beat egg whites (at room temperature) until stiff peaks form; fold into batter.

Pour batter into 3 greased and floured 9-inch round cakepans. Bake at 350° for 30 to 35 minutes or until a wooden pick inserted in center comes out clean. Cool in pans 10 minutes; remove from pans, and cool completely.

Spread Coconut-Pecan Frosting between layers and on top and sides of cake. Garnish with pecan halves, if desired. Yield: one 3-layer cake.

COCONUT-PECAN FROSTING:

1⅓ cups evaporated milk
1½ cups sugar
4 egg yolks
¾ cup butter or margarine
1 teaspoon vanilla extract
1½ cups flaked coconut
¾ cup chopped pecans

Combine milk, sugar, egg yolks, and butter in a heavy saucepan; bring to a boil, and cook over medium heat 12 minutes, stirring constantly. Add vanilla, coconut, and pecans; stir until frosting is cool and of spreading consistency. Yield: enough for one 3-layer cake.

Mrs. Archie David,
Terrell, Tex.

MARBLE CHOCOLATE CHIP CUPCAKES

1 (8-ounce) package cream cheese, softened
1½ cups sugar, divided
1 egg, slightly beaten
⅛ teaspoon salt
1 (6-ounce) package semisweet chocolate morsels
1½ cups all-purpose flour
1 teaspoon soda
½ teaspoon salt
¼ cup cocoa
1 cup water
½ cup vegetable oil
1 tablespoon vinegar
1 teaspoon vanilla extract

Combine cream cheese and ½ cup sugar; beat until smooth. Add egg, ⅛ teaspoon salt, and chocolate morsels, stirring until mixed. Set aside.

Combine flour, remaining 1 cup sugar, soda, ½ teaspoon salt, and cocoa; stir until blended. Add water, oil, vinegar, and vanilla; stir until batter is smooth. Spoon batter into paper-lined muffin cups, filling half full. Spoon a tablespoonful of cream cheese mixture into center of each cupcake. Bake at 350° for 25 to 30 minutes or until cupcakes test done. Yield: 1½ dozen.

Mrs. Jack O'Bryan,
Moberly, Mo.

Tip: Make homemade candy from leftover cake frosting by mixing it with shredded coconut or chopped nuts. Shape into balls and place on waxed paper to harden.

CARROT CAKE

3 eggs
2 cups sugar
1¼ cups vegetable oil
3 cups all-purpose flour
2 teaspoons soda
1 teaspoon salt
2 teaspoons ground cinnamon
1½ cups grated carrot
1 cup chopped pecans
1 (20-ounce) can crushed pineapple, well
    drained
2 teaspoons vanilla extract

Combine eggs, sugar, and oil in a large mixing bowl and mix well. Gradually beat in flour, soda, salt, and cinnamon. Stir in carrot, pecans, pineapple, and vanilla. Pour batter into a greased and floured 10-inch tube pan. Bake at 350° for 1 hour and 15 minutes or until a wooden pick inserted in center comes out clean. Cool 15 to 20 minutes; remove from pan. Yield: one 10-inch cake.   *Phyllis England,*
Deer Lodge, Tenn.

COCONUT-SOUR CREAM CAKE

1 (18.5-ounce) package regular white cake
    mix (not pudding type)
¼ cup vegetable oil
3 eggs
1 (8.5-ounce) can cream of coconut
1 (8-ounce) carton commercial sour cream
Cream Cheese Frosting
1 (3½-ounce) can flaked cocount

Combine first 5 ingredients; beat 2 minutes on high speed of electric mixer. Reduce speed to low; beat 1 minute. Pour batter into a greased and floured 13- x 9 x 2-inch baking pan; bake at 350° for 40 minutes or until a wooden pick inserted in center comes out clean. Let cake cool completely in pan.

Spread Cream Cheese Frosting over cake; sprinkle with coconut. Yield: 15 to 18 servings.

CREAM CHEESE FROSTING:

1 (8-ounce) package cream cheese, softened
2 tablespoons milk
1 (16-ounce) package powdered sugar, sifted
1 teaspoon vanilla extract

Beat cream cheese until light and fluffy; gradually add remaining ingredients, beating well. Yield: enough frosting for one 13- x 9- x 2-inch cake.   *Wilma Sparkman,*
Cleveland, Ark.

REGAL FRUITCAKE

1 (8-ounce) package candied red cherries,
    chopped
1 (8-ounce) package candied green cherries,
    chopped
1½ cups coarsely chopped pecans
1 (7-ounce) can flaked coconut
4¼ cups all-purpose flour, divided
1¼ cups butter or margarine, softened
2 cups sugar
6 eggs
2 teaspoons baking powder
½ teaspoon salt
½ cup orange juice

Combine first 4 ingredients; dredge with ¼ cup flour, stirring to coat well. Set aside.

Cream butter in a large mixing bowl; gradually add sugar, beating until light and fluffy. Add eggs, one at a time, beating well after each addition. Combine remaining flour, baking powder, and salt; add to creamed mixture alternately with orange juice, beginning and ending with flour mixture. Stir in fruit mixture.

Line a greased 10-inch tube pan with brown paper; grease the brown paper. (Do not use recycled brown paper.) Bake at 300° for 2½ hours or until a wooden pick inserted in center comes out clean. Cool cake in pan 20 minutes before removing from pan; peel paper liner from cake. Cool completely on a wire rack. Yield: one 10-inch cake.   *Pearl Bradley,*
Lampasas, Tex.

WHITE FRUITCAKE

1 pound butter, softened
2 cups sugar
6 eggs, separated
1 (15-ounce) package golden raisins
1 cup diced candied pineapple
1½ cups diced candied red cherries
1½ cups diced candied green cherries
1 cup flaked coconut
1 pound pecans, finely chopped
4 cups all-purpose flour, divided
1 (2-ounce) bottle lemon extract
Honey
Additional candied red and green cherries
(optional)

Cream butter and sugar until light and fluffy. Add egg yolks, one at a time, beating well after each addition. Combine fruit, coconut, pecans, and ½ cup flour; mix well. Add fruit mixture to creamed mixture; stir to blend. Stir in remaining flour and lemon extract. Beat egg whites (at room temperature) until stiff; fold into batter.

Spoon batter into a well-greased 10-inch tube pan. Bake at 300° for 2½ to 3 hours or until cake tests done. Brush with honey 30 minutes before cake is done. Decorate top with additional candied fruit when cake is done, if desired. Yield: one 10-inch cake.

Deborah D. Pettit,
Mineral, Va.

BUTTERMILK POUND CAKE

1¼ cups shortening
3 cups sugar
6 eggs
3 cups sifted cake flour, divided
1 cup buttermilk
¼ teaspoon soda
¼ teaspoon salt
½ teaspoon lemon extract
½ teaspoon vanilla extract
3 or 4 drops butter flavoring

Combine shortening and sugar; cream with an electric mixer until light and fluffy. Add eggs, one at a time, beating 30 seconds after each addition.

Stir 1 cup flour into creamed mixture until blended. Combine buttermilk, soda, salt, lemon extract, vanilla extract, and butter flavoring; stir one-half of buttermilk mixture into creamed mixture until blended. Stir 1 cup flour into creamed mixture. Repeat procedure, ending with flour.

Pour batter into a well-greased and floured 10-inch tube pan. Bake at 325° for 1½ hours. Cool 10 to 15 minutes; remove from pan. Yield: one 10-inch cake.

Betty Ann Hayes,
Willacoochee, Ga.

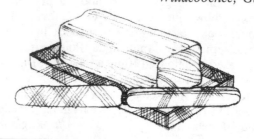

SUNSHINE POUND CAKE

1 cup butter, softened
½ cup shortening
2 cups sugar
5 eggs
3 cups all-purpose flour
1 cup lemon-lime carbonated beverage
2 teaspoons vanilla extract
1 teaspoon lemon extract

Cream butter and shortening; gradually add sugar, beating until light and fluffy. Add eggs, one at a time, beating well after each addition. Add flour, alternately with lemon-lime beverage, mixing well after each addition. Stir in flavorings.

Pour batter into a greased and floured 10-inch Bundt pan; bake at 325° for 1½ hours or until a wooden pick inserted in center comes out clean. Cool in pan 10 to 15 minutes; remove from pan, and cool completely. Yield: one 10-inch cake.

Dorothy Burgess,
Huntsville, Tex.

SOUR CREAM POUND CAKE

1 cup butter or margarine, softened
2½ cups sugar
6 eggs
3 cups all-purpose flour
¼ teaspoon soda
1 (8-ounce) carton commercial sour cream
1 teaspoon vanilla extract
1 teaspoon lemon extract

Cream butter; gradually add sugar, beating until light and fluffy. Add eggs, one at a time, beating well after each addition.

Combine flour and soda; add to creamed mixture alternately with sour cream, mixing well after each addition. Stir in flavorings.

Pour batter into a greased and floured 10-inch tube pan. Bake at 350° for 1 hour and 15 minutes or until a wooden pick inserted in center comes out clean. Cool in pan 10 minutes; remove from pan, and cool completely. Yield: one 10-inch cake.   *Mrs. J. A. Copeland,*
Valdosta, Ga.

EASY HARVEST PEANUT CAKE

¼ cup instant nonfat dry milk powder
¾ cup water
1 cup creamy peanut butter
⅔ cup butter, softened
2 cups firmly packed brown sugar
6 eggs
2 cups all-purpose flour
2 teaspoons baking powder
½ teaspoon salt
2 teaspoons vanilla extract
Peanut Butter Frosting
½ cup chopped roasted peanuts

Add dry milk powder to water, stirring until dissolved; set aside.

Cream peanut butter and butter. Gradually add sugar, beating well. Add eggs, one at a time, beating well after each addition.

Combine flour, baking powder, and salt; add to creamed mixture alternately with milk mixture, beating well after each addition. Stir in vanilla.

Pour batter into a greased and floured 13- x 9- x 2-inch baking pan. Bake at 350° for 45 minutes or until wooden pick inserted in center comes out clean. Cool cake in pan completely. Spread Peanut Butter Frosting on top of cake. Sprinkle with peanuts. Cut into squares. Yield: one 13- x 9- x 2-inch cake.

PEANUT BUTTER FROSTING:

½ cup creamy peanut butter
1 (16-ounce) package powdered sugar, sifted
½ cup plus 1 tablespoon milk
1 teaspoon vanilla extract

Cream peanut butter; gradually add half of sugar, beating well. Add remaining sugar alternately with milk, beating until smooth enough to spread. Add vanilla; beat well. Yield: enough for one 13- x 9- x 2-inch cake.

Donna White,
Ashford, Ala.

APPLE BUTTER BARS

1½ cups all-purpose flour
1 teaspoon soda
1 teaspoon salt
2½ cups quick-cooking oats, uncooked
1½ cups sugar
1 cup butter or margarine, melted
1½ cups apple butter

Combine flour, soda, and salt in a large bowl; add oats and sugar. Stir in butter and mix well. Press half of mixture into a greased 13- x 9- x 2-inch baking pan; top with apple butter. Sprinkle with remaining crumb mixture; press gently with a spoon.

Bake at 350° for 55 minutes or until browned. Cool; cut into bars. Yield: 3 dozen.
Melody Gourley,
Alamo, Tenn.

HAWAIIAN BARS

¼ cup butter or margarine, softened
1 cup firmly packed light brown sugar
1½ cups flaked coconut
1 cup all-purpose flour
½ teaspoon salt
Pineapple Filling

Cream butter and brown sugar until light and fluffy. Add coconut, flour, and salt; mix with a fork until crumbly.

Press half of crumb mixture into a greased 9-inch square baking pan. Spread Pineapple Filling evenly over crumb mixture. Cover with remaining crumb mixture and gently press down. Bake at 350° for 30 to 35 minutes. Yield: about 4 dozen.

PINEAPPLE FILLING:

1 (8-ounce) can crushed pineapple,
    undrained
¾ cup sugar
3 tablespoons cornstarch
¼ teaspoon salt
1 tablespoon butter or margarine
1 tablespoon lemon juice

Combine pineapple, sugar, cornstarch, and salt in a medium saucepan, stirring to mix. Bring to a boil and cook, stirring constantly, about 5 minutes or until thickened. Remove from heat and stir in butter and lemon juice. Allow to cool slightly. Yield: about ¾ cup.

Harletta Carthel,
Gruver, Tex.

LEMON CHESS BARS

2¼ cups all-purpose flour, divided
1 cup butter, softened
½ cup sifted powdered sugar
1 teaspoon baking powder
4 eggs, beaten
2 cups sugar
1 teaspoon grated lemon rind
¼ cup lemon juice

Combine 2 cups flour, butter, and powdered sugar, mixing well. Pat evenly into a 13- x 9- x 2-inch pan, pressing mixture about ¼ inch up sides of pan. Bake at 350° for 20 minutes.

Combine remaining ¼ cup flour and baking powder; add remaining ingredients, mixing well. Pour over hot crust. Bake at 350° for 25 minutes. Cool; cut into bars. Yield: 2 dozen.

Margot Foster,
Hubbard, Tex.

NUTTY DATE BARS

1 cup all-purpose flour
½ cup butter or margarine, softened
1 teaspoon vanilla extract, divided
2 eggs
1 cup firmly packed brown sugar
1 cup chopped dates
1 cup chopped pecans
⅓ cup orange marmalade
2 tablespoons all-purpose flour
½ teaspoon baking powder
¼ teaspoon salt

Combine flour, butter, and ½ teaspoon vanilla; blend with pastry cutter until mixture forms a soft dough. Press into a greased 11- x 7- x 2-inch baking pan. Bake at 350° for 12 to 15 minutes or until lightly browned.

Beat eggs until frothy in a small mixing bowl. Stir in remaining ingredients; mix well. Spread on pastry layer. Bake 25 to 30 minutes or until top is set and browned. Cool; cut into bars. Yield: 2 dozen.   *Frances Whitehead,*
Big Lake, Tex.

PEANUT BUTTER LOGS

1 (16-ounce) package powdered sugar, sifted
3 cups crisp rice cereal
2 cups crunchy peanut butter
½ cup butter or margarine
1 (6-ounce) package semisweet chocolate
    morsels
1 (6-ounce) package butterscotch morsels
Decorator sprinkles (optional)

Combine sugar and cereal in a large mixing bowl; set aside.

Melt peanut butter and butter over low heat in a small saucepan; pour over cereal mixture, mixing well. Roll mixture into 1½- x 1-inch rectangular bars. Chill 1 to 2 hours.

Melt chocolate morsels in top of double boiler, stirring constantly; remove from heat. Place several peanut butter bars in chocolate and roll with a spoon to coat evenly. Remove with spoon, and place on waxed paper to cool. Continue process until half the peanut butter bars are covered.

Melt butterscotch morsels in top of double boiler, stirring constantly. Remove from heat and repeat above procedure with remaining peanut butter bars. Top with decorator sprinkles, if desired. Yield: about 5 dozen.

Deborah Hatton,
Columbia, Ala.

CHERRY WINKS

1 cup shortening
1 (3-ounce) package cream cheese, softened
1 cup sugar
1 egg
1 teaspoon almond extract
2½ cups all-purpose flour
¼ teaspoon soda
½ teaspoon salt
1¼ cups finely chopped pecans
36 maraschino cherries, halved

Cream shortening and cream cheese; gradually add sugar, beating until light and fluffy. Add egg and almond extract; beat well.

Combine flour, soda, and salt; add to creamed mixture, beating well. Chill mixture about 1 hour.

Shape dough into 1-inch balls; roll in pecans. Place on ungreased cookie sheets; press a cherry half into the center of each cookie. Bake at 350° for 12 to 15 minutes. Yield: about 6 dozen.

Wilma L. Hamaker,
Banks, Ark.

CARROT COOKIES

½ cup shortening
½ cup butter or margarine, softened
¾ cup sugar
2 eggs
1¼ cups cooked mashed carrots
2 cups all-purpose flour
2 teaspoons baking powder
¼ teaspoon salt
1 cup flaked coconut
½ cup finely chopped pecans

Combine shortening, butter, and sugar in a large mixing bowl; cream until light and fluffy. Add eggs and carrots, mixing well.

Combine flour, baking powder, and salt; add to creamed mixture and stir well. Stir in coconut and pecans. Drop dough by teaspoonfuls onto greased cookie sheets. Bake at 400° for 10 to 12 minutes or until firm. Cool on wire racks. Yield: about 7 dozen.

Cindy Tippett,
Shreveport, La.

GINGER CRINKLES

⅔ cup vegetable oil
1¼ cups sugar, divided
1 egg
¼ cup molasses
2 cups all-purpose flour
½ teaspoon salt
2 teaspoons soda
1 teaspoon ground cinnamon
1 teaspoon ground ginger

Combine oil and 1 cup sugar in a large mixing bowl; add egg and beat well. Stir in molasses. Combine flour, salt, soda, cinnamon, and ginger; add to molasses mixture, stirring well. Roll dough into 1-inch balls; roll each in remaining ¼ cup sugar. Place 2 inches apart on greased cookie sheets. Bake at 350° for 10 to 12 minutes or until lightly browned. Remove to wire rack to cool. Yield: about 4 dozen.

Sue Ellen Buchanan,
Jackson, Ala.

DUTCH SOUR CREAM COOKIES

½ cup butter or margarine, softened
1 cup sugar
1 egg
½ teaspoon orange or lemon extract
½ teaspoon vanilla extract
3 cups all-purpose flour
¼ teaspoon soda
¼ cup commercial sour cream

Cream butter; gradually add sugar, beating until light and fluffy. Add egg and flavorings; beat well.

Combine flour and soda; add to creamed mixture alternately with sour cream, beating just until blended.

Shape dough into a long roll, 2 inches in diameter; wrap in waxed paper, and chill 2 to 3 hours or until firm. Unwrap roll and cut into ¼-inch slices; place on ungreased cookie sheets. Bake at 375° for 8 to 10 minutes. Yield: 4 dozen.

Melissa Walker,
Maryville, Tenn.

MIRACLE COOKIES

1 cup peanut butter
1 cup sugar
1 egg, beaten
1 teaspoon vanilla extract

Combine peanut butter and sugar; mix well. Stir in egg and vanilla. Roll dough into ¾-inch balls. Place on ungreased cookie sheets. Flatten with a floured fork.

Bake at 350° for 10 minutes. Allow to cool before removing from cookie sheet. Yield: about 4 dozen.

Carolyn Stewart,
Collinsville, Okla.

Tip: Stale cake or cookies can be made into crumbs in a blender. Sprinkle over ice cream for a delicious topping.

FUDGE JAVA

3 cups sugar
Dash of salt
½ cup half-and-half
2 tablespoons instant coffee powder
2 tablespoons light corn syrup
1 cup milk
3 tablespoons butter or margarine
1 teaspoon vanilla extract

Combine first 6 ingredients in a heavy 3-quart saucepan; cook over low heat, stirring constantly, until sugar is dissolved. Continue cooking, without stirring, until mixture reaches soft ball stage (234°). Remove from heat, and add butter and vanilla (do not stir). Cool mixture to lukewarm (110°).

Beat on medium speed of an electric mixer until mixture begins to thicken. Pour into a buttered 8-inch square pan. Cool completely. Cut into 1-inch squares. Yield: about 5 dozen.

Kathy Young,
Clarksville, Tenn.

BUTTERSCOTCH MERINGUE PIE

1 cup firmly packed brown sugar
1 tablespoon plus 1 teaspoon sugar
¼ cup all-purpose flour
⅛ teaspoon salt
1½ cups milk
¼ cup butter or margarine, melted
2 eggs, separated
1 teaspoon vanilla extract
1 baked 8-inch pastry shell
¼ cup sugar

Combine sugar, flour, and salt in the top of a double boiler; add milk and butter, stirring well. Cook over boiling water, stirring constantly, until mixture is thickened (about 30 minutes).

Beat egg yolks until thick and lemon colored. Stir a small amount of hot mixture into yolks; stir yolks into remaining hot mixture.

Cover and cook 15 minutes over boiling water, stirring frequently. Remove from heat; stir in vanilla. Cool; pour into pastry shell.

Beat egg whites (at room temperature) until frothy in a small mixing bowl. Gradually add ¼ cup sugar; continue beating until stiff peaks form. Spread meringue over filling, sealing to edge of pastry. Bake at 425° for 6 to 8 minutes or until lightly browned. Cool. Refrigerate pie until chilled. Yield: one 8-inch pie.
Mrs. Willis J. Dewar,
Selma, N.C.

pastry edge with aluminum foil to prevent excessive browning. Bake 10 minutes longer or until pie is set. Cool on a wire rack. Yield: one 9-inch pie.
Mrs. Raymond Simpson,
Cleveland, Tenn.

BUTTERMILK PIE

1⅓ cups sugar
3 tablespoons all-purpose flour
2 eggs, beaten
½ cup butter or margarine, melted
1 cup buttermilk
2 teaspoons vanilla extract
1 teaspoon lemon extract
1 unbaked 9-inch pastry shell

Combine sugar and flour, mixing well; add eggs, butter, and buttermilk. Beat well. Stir in flavorings. Pour into pastry shell. Bake at 400° for 10 minutes. Reduce heat and bake at 325° for 30 to 35 minutes. Yield: one 9-inch pie.
Varniece Warren,
Hermitage, Ark.

EASY CHOCOLATE PIE

1 cup sugar
3 tablespoons cornstarch
Dash of salt
2 cups milk
3 eggs, separated
1 (1-ounce) square unsweetened chocolate
1 tablespoon butter or margarine
1 teaspoon vanilla extract
1 baked 9-inch pastry shell
½ teaspoon cream of tartar
¼ cup plus 2 tablespoons sugar

Combine 1 cup sugar, cornstarch, and salt in a heavy saucepan; mix well.

Combine milk and egg yolks; beat with a wire whisk 1 to 2 minutes or until frothy. Gradually stir into sugar mixture, mixing well. Place over medium heat and stir constantly until thickened and bubbly. Remove from heat; add chocolate, butter, and vanilla, stirring until chocolate and butter melt. Pour into pastry shell; set aside.

Beat egg whites (at room temperature) until frothy; add cream of tartar, beating slightly. Gradually add ¼ cup plus 2 tablespoons sugar, 1 tablespoon at a time, beating until stiff peaks form. Spread meringue over filling, sealing to edge of pastry. Bake at 350° for 10 to 12 minutes or until golden brown. Yield: one 9-inch pie.
Bonita Loewe,
Carmine, Tex.

BUTTERMILK-LEMON PIE

3 eggs
1½ cups sugar
½ cup buttermilk
3 tablespoons butter or margarine, melted
1 tablespoon all-purpose flour
2 tablespoons lemon juice
1 teaspoon lemon extract
1 unbaked 9-inch pastry shell

Beat eggs in a medium mixing bowl; add next 6 ingredients, and mix well. Pour into pastry shell. Bake at 425° for 10 minutes. Cover

CHOCOLATE MOCHA CRUNCH PIE

½ cup butter or margarine, softened
¾ cup firmly packed brown sugar
1 (1-ounce) square unsweetened chocolate, melted and cooled
2 teaspoons instant coffee granules
2 eggs
Mocha Pie Shell
2 cups whipping cream
½ cup sifted powdered sugar
1½ tablespoons instant coffee granules
½ square semisweet chocolate, grated (optional)

Place butter in a small mixing bowl and beat until creamy. Gradually add brown sugar and beat at medium speed of electric mixer 2 to 3 minutes, scraping sides of bowl occasionally. Stir in 1 square melted chocolate and 2 teaspoons coffee granules. Add eggs, one at a time, beating 5 minutes after each addition. Pour filling into Mocha Pie Shell. Refrigerate at least 6 hours or overnight.

About 1 or 2 hours before serving, combine cream, powdered sugar, and 1½ tablespoons coffee granules in a large, chilled mixing bowl. Beat cream until stiff (do not overbeat). Spoon over chilled filling. Sprinkle with ½ square grated semisweet chocolate, if desired. Chill. Yield: one 9-inch pie.

MOCHA PIE SHELL:

1 piecrust stick, crumbled
1 (1-ounce) square unsweetened chocolate, grated
¾ cup finely chopped walnuts or pecans
¼ cup firmly packed brown sugar
1 tablespoon water
1 teaspoon vanilla extract

Use a fork to combine crumbled piecrust stick and chocolate in a medium bowl. Stir in walnuts and sugar. Combine water and vanilla; sprinkle over pastry mixture. Mix with fork until mixture forms a ball.

Line a 9-inch piepan with aluminum foil; place a circle of waxed paper over foil in the bottom of piepan. Press pastry mixture evenly into piepan.

Bake at 375° for 15 minutes; cool completely. Invert crust on an 8½-inch piepan; remove foil and waxed paper. Return to 9-inch piepan. Yield: one 9-inch pie shell.

Mrs. Warren D. Davis,
Yulee, Fla.

LEMON CHEESE PIE

1 (3-ounce) package lemon-flavored gelatin
1 cup boiling water
3 tablespoons lemon juice
1 (8-ounce) package cream cheese, softened
1 cup sugar
1 teaspoon vanilla extract
1 (13-ounce) can evaporated milk, chilled
2 (9-inch) graham cracker crusts

Dissolve gelatin in boiling water; stir in lemon juice and set aside to cool.

Combine cream cheese, sugar, and vanilla; cream until light and fluffy. Add cooled gelatin mixture; mix until smooth. Beat milk in a large chilled mixing bowl until stiff peaks form. Stir in cheese mixture. Spoon filling into two 9-inch graham cracker crusts. Chill at least 3 hours. Yield: two 9-inch pies. *Elaine Bell,*
Dexter, N. Mex.

HEAVENLY PIE

4 eggs, separated
¼ teaspoon cream of tartar
1½ cups sugar, divided
1 tablespoon grated lemon rind
3 tablespoons fresh lemon juice
⅛ teaspoon salt
2 cups whipping cream, whipped

Beat egg whites (at room temperature) until frothy; add cream of tartar, beating slightly. Gradually add 1 cup sugar, beating well after each addition; continue beating until stiff peaks form. Do not underbeat.

Spoon meringue into a well-greased 9-inch pieplate. Use a spoon to shape meringue into a pie shell, swirling sides high. Bake at 275° for 50 minutes. Cool.

Beat egg yolks until thick and lemon colored. Gradually add remaining sugar, lemon rind, lemon juice, and salt. Cook in top of a double boiler, stirring constantly, until smooth and thickened. Cool.

Fold half of whipped cream into lemon mixture; spoon into meringue shell and spread evenly. Cover and refrigerate at least 12 hours. Top with remaining whipped cream. Yield: one 9-inch pie.   *Mrs. Warren D. Davis,*
Yulee, Fla.

CREAMY PEANUT BUTTER PIE

2 (3-ounce) packages cream cheese, softened
1 (12-ounce) container frozen whipped
    topping, thawed
1 cup crunchy peanut butter
1 cup sifted powdered sugar
3 tablespoons milk
1 (9-inch) graham cracker crust
Chopped roasted peanuts (optional)

Beat cream cheese at high speed of electric mixer until fluffy. Add whipped topping, peanut butter, sugar, and milk; beat well. Spoon into graham cracker crust. Chill at least 5 hours before serving. Garnish with peanuts, if desired. Yield: one 9-inch pie. *Shea Woodham,*
Newton, Ala.

TEXAS PECAN PIE

⅓ cup butter or margarine, melted
1 cup sugar
1 cup light corn syrup
½ teaspoon salt
2 teaspoons vanilla extract
4 eggs, slightly beaten
1 cup coarsely chopped pecans
1 unbaked 9-inch pastry shell

Combine butter, sugar, corn syrup, salt, and vanilla in a medium mixing bowl; beat well.

Add eggs, mixing well. Stir in pecans. Pour into pastry shell. Bake at 375° for 45 to 50 minutes. Yield: one 9-inch pie.   *Flora Bowie,*
Splendora, Tex.

FRIED APPLE PIES

1 (8-ounce) package dried apples
2 tablespoons butter or margarine, melted
½ to 1 cup sugar
1 teaspoon ground cinnamon
2 tablespoons lemon juice
Buttermilk Pastry (recipe follows)
Vegetable oil

Place apples in a saucepan; cover with water. Bring to a boil; reduce heat and simmer, uncovered, 15 to 20 minutes or until apples are tender. Add butter, sugar, cinnamon, and lemon juice; mash well.

Divide pastry into 3 equal portions; roll out on waxed paper. Cut out pastry circles, using a 5-inch saucer as a measure. Place about 3 tablespoons of apple mixture on half of each pastry circle. To seal, dip fingers in water and moisten edges of circles; fold in half, making sure edges are even. Using a fork dipped in flour, press pastry edges firmly together.

Heat 1 inch of oil to 375°. Cook pies until golden brown on both sides, turning only once. Drain well on paper towels. Yield: about 1½ dozen.

BUTTERMILK PASTRY:

3 cups all-purpose flour
½ teaspoon soda
1 tablespoon baking powder
⅓ cup shortening
1 egg
1 cup buttermilk

Combine flour, soda, and baking powder; cut in shortening until mixture resembles coarse meal. Combine egg and buttermilk; add to flour mixture. Knead until smooth. Yield: pastry for about 1½ dozen (5-inch) pies.

Lulu B. Worrell,
Hillsville, Va.

LUSCIOUS PEACH PIE

2 (3-ounce) packages cream cheese, softened
¾ cup sifted powdered sugar
¼ teaspoon almond extract
¾ cup whipping cream, whipped
1 (16-ounce) can sliced peaches, drained
1 (9-inch) graham cracker crust

Combine cream cheese, sugar, and almond extract in a medium mixing bowl; cream well. Fold in whipped cream. Gently stir in peaches. Pour filling into graham cracker crust. Chill. Yield: one 9-inch pie.   *Carolyn Gammon,*
Tignall, Ga.

PINEAPPLE MERINGUE PIE

3 eggs, separated
1 cup sugar
¼ cup plus 1 tablespoon all-purpose flour
2 cups crushed pineapple, undrained
1 teaspoon lemon juice
⅛ teaspoon salt
1 tablespoon butter or margarine
1 baked 9-inch pastry shell
1 tablespoon water
¼ teaspoon cream of tartar
¾ teaspoon vanilla extract
¼ cup plus 2 tablespoons sugar

Beat egg yolks until thick and lemon colored. Combine yolks, 1 cup sugar, flour, pineapple, lemon juice, and salt in top of double boiler. Cook over boiling water, stirring constantly, until thickened. Remove from heat and stir in butter. Pour mixture into pastry shell.

Combine egg whites (at room temperature), water, cream of tartar, and vanilla in a small mixing bowl; beat until frothy. Gradually add remaining sugar; continue beating until stiff peaks form. Spread meringue over pie and seal edges carefully. Bake at 400° about 10 minutes or until lightly browned. Cool. Refrigerate pie until chilled. Yield: one 9-inch pie.
Varniece R. Warren,
Hermitage, Ark.

SPAGHETTI SQUASH PIE

1 medium spaghetti squash
2 unbaked 9-inch pastry shells
1½ cups sugar
1 tablespoon cornstarch
½ cup butter or margarine, melted
4 egg yolks, beaten
1 cup milk
2 teaspoons vanilla extract
¼ teaspoon salt
Whipped cream (optional)

Cut squash in half, and discard seeds. Place squash, cut side down, in a large Dutch oven; add 2 inches of water. Bring to a boil, cover and cook 25 to 30 minutes or until squash is tender. Drain squash; cool.

Using a fork, remove spaghetti-like strands from inside squash. Place half of squash strands in each pastry shell; spread strands evenly over bottom.

Combine remaining ingredients, except whipped cream; mix well. Pour half of milk mixture over squash in each pastry shell. Bake at 350° for 30 to 35 minutes or until filling is set. Serve pie warm or cool. Top with whipped cream before serving, if desired. Yield: two 9-inch pies.   *Edna Morgan,*
Canton, Ga.

GREEN TOMATO PIE

1¾ cups sugar
4 to 5 teaspoons all-purpose flour
½ teaspoon ground cinnamon
½ teaspoon ground nutmeg
¼ teaspoon salt
4 cups thinly sliced peeled green tomatoes
2 tablespoons vinegar
Pastry for double-crust 9-inch pie
⅛ teaspoon ground cinnamon
2 teaspoons sugar

Combine first 5 ingredients in a large mixing bowl; stir well. Add tomatoes and vinegar;

stir gently to coat tomatoes. Spoon mixture into a pastry-lined 9-inch pieplate.

Roll out remaining pastry, and carefully place over pie, leaving a 1-inch rim beyond edge of pan. Seal and flute edges; cut several slits in top to allow steam to escape. Combine remaining cinnamon and sugar, and sprinkle over top of pie. Cover pastry edge with aluminum foil to prevent excessive browning. Bake at 425° for 30 minutes. Remove foil and continue baking for 15 to 20 minutes. Yield: one 9-inch pie.

J. S. Walker,
McLouth, Kans.

CHOCOLATE-CHERRY FREEZE

1¼ cups finely crushed vanilla wafers (about 35)
¼ cup butter or margarine, melted
1 quart cherry-nut ice cream, softened
½ cup butter or margarine
2 (1-ounce) squares unsweetened chocolate
3 eggs, separated
1½ cups sifted powdered sugar
1 teaspoon vanilla extract
½ cup chopped pecans

Combine crumbs and melted butter, mixing well. Reserve ¼ cup crumb mixture; press remaining mixture into a 9-inch square baking dish. Spread ice cream over crumb mixture; freeze until firm.

Combine ½ cup butter and chocolate in a saucepan; cook over low heat until melted. Beat egg yolks well, stir in a small amount of chocolate mixture. Combine egg yolks, chocolate, powdered sugar, and vanilla; stir to mix well. Cool thoroughly.

Beat egg whites (at room temperature) until stiff but not dry. Beat chocolate mixture on high speed of electric mixer until light and fluffy. Fold egg whites and pecans into chocolate mixture; spread over ice cream. Sprinkle with reserved ¼ cup crumbs. Freeze. Yield: 8 to 10 servings.

Shirley Sump,
Clay Center, Kans.

FREEZING PEACHES

Select firm, ripe peaches; sort and wash. Peel, then halve or slice. Prepare in one of the following ways:

Sugar pack: Mix ⅔ cup sugar and ¼ teaspoon ascorbic-citric mixture for each quart of fruit. Sprinkle peaches with sugar-ascorbic mixture; allow to stand about 10 minutes or until sugar dissolves.

Pack peaches to the fill line in freezer containers, allowing at least ¾-inch headspace. Crumple a piece of moistureproof, vaporproof paper and place over peaches. Wipe rim of container; seal, label, and freeze.

Syrup pack: Combine 3 cups sugar and 4 cups water; bring to a boil, stirring until sugar dissolves. This makes about 5½ cups of syrup. You will need about ⅔ cup of syrup for each pint container of peaches. Allow syrup to cool completely. Stir in ½ teaspoon ascorbic-citric mixture for each quart of syrup.

Place peaches in freezer containers. Press fruit down and add syrup to cover, leaving at least ¾-inch headspace. Crumple a piece of moistureproof, vaporproof paper and place over peaches. Wipe rim of container; seal, label, and freeze.

CREAMY PEACH FREEZE

1 (1½-ounce) package whipped topping mix
1 (16-ounce) can sliced peaches, drained

Prepare whipped topping mix according to package directions. Combine whipped topping and peaches in container of electric blender; process until smooth. Spoon into 4 serving dishes; freeze 2 to 3 hours or until firm. Remove from freezer 5 minutes before serving. Yield: 4 servings.

Marie Raney,
Dogpatch, Ark.

Tip: If a recipe calls for beaten egg whites, beat them first and then use beaters without washing for beating egg yolks. Saves on cleanup.

BERRIES ON SNOW

2 cups graham cracker crumbs
½ cup butter or margarine, softened
3 tablespoons powdered sugar
1 (2.5-ounce) package whipped topping mix
1 cup sugar
1 cup cold milk
1 teaspoon vanilla extract
1 (8-ounce) package cream cheese, softened
1 (3-ounce) package cream cheese, softened
1 (21-ounce) can blueberry or cherry pie
    filling

Combine graham cracker crumbs, butter, and powdered sugar, mixing well; press into bottom and ½ inch up sides of a 13- x 9- x 2-inch baking pan. Bake at 350° for 5 minutes. Cool.

Combine whipped topping mix, sugar, milk, and vanilla in a large mixing bowl. Beat until soft peaks form (about 2 minutes). Gradually add both packages of cream cheese, beating until smooth and well blended. Spread over crust; chill about 30 minutes. Spread pie filling evenly over cream cheese layer; chill several hours or overnight. Store in refrigerator. Yield: about 15 servings.
Eva Crockett Carter,
Rose Hill, Va.

BROWNIE MINT DESSERT

3 egg whites
¾ cup sugar
¾ cup chocolate wafer crumbs
½ cup chopped walnuts or pecans
½ teaspoon vanilla extract
1 cup whipping cream
2 tablespoons powdered sugar
¼ cup crushed soft peppermint stick candy
Chocolate curls
Grated chocolate

Beat egg whites (at room temperature) until frothy. Gradually add sugar, 1 tablespoon at a time, beating until mixture is glossy. Fold in crumbs, walnuts, and vanilla. Spread mixture into a buttered 8-inch square baking dish. Bake at 325° for 30 minutes. Cool.

Beat whipping cream until foamy; gradually add powdered sugar, beating until soft peaks form. Fold in peppermint; spread over chocolate layer. Garnish with chocolate curls and grated chocolate. Cover and chill at least 3 hours. Cut into squares to serve. Store in refrigerator. Yield: 9 servings.
Mrs. Lake A. Anderson,
Old Fort, N.C.

FROSTY FRUIT MEDLEY

1 (10-ounce) package frozen mixed fruit,
    thawed
2 bananas, peeled and sliced
¼ cup commercial sour cream
2 tablespoons brown sugar

Combine mixed fruit and bananas; mix gently. Cover and chill. Just before serving, spoon fruit mixture into individual serving dishes. Top each with sour cream and sprinkle with brown sugar. Yield: 4 servings.
Mrs. H. C. Quesenberry,
Dugspur, Va.

LEMON DELIGHT

½ cup butter or margarine
1 cup all-purpose flour
¾ cup chopped pecans or walnuts, divided
1 (8-ounce) package cream cheese, softened
1 cup sifted powdered sugar
3 cups frozen whipped topping, thawed and
    divided
2 (3¾-ounce) packages lemon instant pudding
    and pie filling mix
3 cups milk

Cut butter into flour until mixture resembles coarse meal; stir ½ cup pecans into flour mixture. Press pecan mixture into a 13- x 9- x 2-inch baking pan. Bake at 350° for 15 minutes.

Combine cream cheese and powdered sugar; beat until fluffy. Fold 1 cup whipped topping into cream cheese mixture. Spread over crust; chill.

Combine pudding mix and milk; beat 2 minutes on low speed of electric mixer. Spread pudding over cream cheese layer. Spread remaining whipped topping over pudding layer. Sprinkle with remaining pecans. Chill. Store in refrigerator. Yield: about 15 servings.

Mrs. Guy Williams,
Greenville, S.C.

FRESH PEACH ICE CREAM

6 to 8 medium peaches, peeled and mashed
2 cups sugar
2 (13-ounce) cans evaporated milk
1 (12-ounce) can apricot nectar

Combine all ingredients in a large bowl; stir until sugar is dissolved.

Pour mixture into freezer can of a 1-gallon hand-turned or electric freezer. Freeze according to manufacturer's instructions. Let ripen at least 1 hour. Yield: about 1 gallon.

Dorothy Anderson,
Manor, Tex.

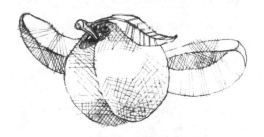

CRUSTY PEACH CUPS

3 medium peaches, peeled and halved
2 eggs
¾ cup sugar
½ teaspoon ground cinnamon
2 cups soft breadcrumbs
2 tablespoons butter or margarine, melted

Place each peach half, cut side up, in a greased 10-ounce custard cup. Beat eggs until light and fluffy; gradually add sugar, beating constantly. Stir in cinnamon, breadcrumbs, and butter. Spoon breadcrumb mixture evenly over peaches. Bake at 400° for 20 to 25 minutes. Yield: 6 servings. *Sue Garrett,*
Tuscumbia, Ala.

PEACH CRISP

2 cups sliced fresh or canned peaches
¼ cup butter or margarine, softened
1¾ cups sugar, divided
1 cup all-purpose flour
1 teaspoon baking powder
½ teaspoon salt
½ cup milk
1 tablespoon cornstarch
¼ teaspoon ground nutmeg
1 cup boiling water
Whipping cream or ice cream (optional)

Place peach slices in an 8-inch square baking pan.

Cream butter and ¾ cup sugar. Combine flour, baking powder, and salt; add to creamed mixture alternately with milk. Spoon mixture over fruit.

Sift together 1 cup sugar, cornstarch, and nutmeg; sprinkle over batter. Pour boiling water over top. Bake at 350° for 1 hour. Serve with whipping cream or ice cream, if desired. Yield: 6 servings. *Anna D. Swan,*
Louisville, Ky.

CRANBERRY-APPLE CRUNCH

2 cups fresh cranberries
3 cups chopped, unpeeled tart apple
1 cup sugar
½ cup firmly packed brown sugar
¼ cup all-purpose flour
½ cup butter or margarine, softened
1 cup uncooked regular oats
1 cup pecans, chopped

Combine cranberries, apple, and sugar in a lightly greased, shallow 1½-quart casserole.

Combine brown sugar and flour; cut in butter with a pastry blender until mixture resembles coarse crumbs. Stir in oats and pecans. Sprinkle mixture over cranberries. Bake at 375° for 1 hour or until golden brown. Yield: 5 to 6 servings.

LEMON PUDDING

1 cup sugar
3 tablespoons all-purpose flour
Pinch of salt
Grated rind of 1 lemon
Juice of 1 lemon
1 egg yolk, beaten
1 cup milk
1 tablespoon vegetable oil
2 egg whites

Combine sugar, flour, salt, lemon rind, and juice in a large mixing bowl; mix well. Stir in egg yolk, milk, and oil. Beat egg whites (at room temperature) until stiff but not dry; fold into lemon mixture. Pour into a greased 1½-quart casserole. Pour 1 to 1½ inches water in a baking pan, and place casserole in pan. Bake at 350° for 45 minutes or until edges are lightly browned. Yield: 6 servings.

ORANGE PUDDING

1 tablespoon unflavored gelatin
½ cup orange juice
½ cup sugar
1 tablespoon all-purpose flour
3 eggs, separated
1 cup milk, scalded
1 tablespoon butter or margarine
Grated rind of 1 orange
About 13 ladyfingers, split
Whipped cream

Combine gelatin and orange juice; set aside. Combine sugar and flour in a medium saucepan; set aside. Beat egg yolks until thick and lemon colored, and add to sugar mixture. Stir in milk and butter. Cook, stirring constantly, over low heat until mixture coats a spoon. Stir in gelatin mixture and orange rind. Beat egg whites (at room temperature) until soft peaks form; fold into pudding.

Line a greased 2-quart dish with ladyfingers; spoon pudding into lined dish. Chill several hours until set. Serve with whipped cream. Yield: 6 to 8 servings.

OLDTIME BREAD PUDDING

4 slices buttered toast, cut into quarters
⅓ cup raisins
2 eggs, slightly beaten
1 tablespoon plus 2 teaspoons sugar, divided
⅛ teaspoon salt
1 cup milk
1 cup boiling water
1 teaspoon vanilla extract
¼ teaspoon ground cinnamon

Place toast in a greased 1½-quart casserole; sprinkle with raisins. Combine eggs, 4 teaspoons sugar, salt, milk, water, and vanilla; pour over toast. Let stand 10 minutes; sprinkle with cinnamon and remaining sugar. Bake at 350° for 30 to 40 minutes or until a knife inserted in the center comes out clean. Yield: 4 to 6 servings.

RAISIN BREAD PUDDING

1 (16-ounce) loaf raisin bread, cubed
4 eggs
½ cup sugar
4 cups milk
2 teaspoons vanilla extract
2 to 3 tablespoons butter or margarine
Vanilla ice cream

Place bread cubes in a greased 13- x 9- x 2-inch pan; set aside. Combine eggs, sugar, milk, and vanilla; pour over bread cubes. Dot with butter. Bake at 350° about 55 minutes or until knife inserted in center comes out clean. Serve warm or cold with vanilla ice cream. Yield: about 8 servings.

For a cake that will complete any feast, select from one of these. Clockwise from top: German Chocolate Cake (page 16), Sour Cream Pound Cake (page 19), Regal Fruitcake (page 17), or Best Ever Chocolate Cake (page 15).

Overleaf: *As an elegant alternative to turkey, serve Fruit-Stuffed Goose (page 44). This delicious bird will add grace to your holiday table.*

Main Dishes

SAUCY STUFFED PEPPERS

8 medium-size green peppers
1 pound ground chuck
1¼ cups soft breadcrumbs
3 medium onions, chopped
½ cup chopped celery
½ cup catsup
1 egg, beaten
1 teaspoon salt
¼ teaspoon dried parsley flakes
⅛ teaspoon dried whole thyme
⅛ teaspoon poultry seasoning
1 (16-ounce) can whole tomatoes, chopped
    and undrained
1 (8-ounce) can tomato sauce
¼ cup uncooked regular rice
Dash of salt
Dash of sugar

Cut off tops of green peppers; remove stems and seeds. Dice tops and set aside.

Combine ground chuck, breadcrumbs, onion, celery, catsup, egg, 1 teaspoon salt, parsley, thyme, poultry seasoning, and ¼ cup reserved diced green pepper; stir well. Fill peppers with meat mixture; place in a 13- x 9- x 2-inch baking pan.

Combine tomatoes, remaining diced pepper, tomato sauce, rice, remaining salt, and sugar; stir well. Pour sauce around peppers. Bake at 350° for 15 minutes; reduce temperature to 325°, and bake an additional 45 minutes. Yield: 8 servings.   *Mrs. H. Lester Hunt,*
Daytona Beach, Fla.

TAMALE CASSEROLE

1 pound ground beef
½ pound bulk sausage
2 cups diced celery
1 cup chopped onion
1 clove garlic, minced (optional)
1 (28-ounce) can tomatoes, undrained
2 cups cooked and drained whole kernel corn
2 teaspoons chili powder
1 teaspoon salt
½ cup cornmeal
1 cup sliced pitted ripe olives
1½ cups (6 ounces) shredded Cheddar cheese

Combine first 5 ingredients in a Dutch oven; cook over medium heat until meat is browned, stirring to crumble meat. Drain; stir in tomatoes, corn, chili powder, and salt. Reduce heat and simmer 15 minutes.

Gradually add cornmeal; cook over low heat until thickened, stirring frequently. Stir in olives; spoon mixture into a lightly greased 2½-quart casserole. Bake at 350° for 40 minutes. Remove from oven and top with cheese; bake an additional 5 minutes or until cheese is melted. Yield: 8 servings.

Note: 1 (17-ounce) can whole kernel corn, drained, may be substituted for 2 cups corn.
Ileen Vannoy,
Uvalde, Tex.

Tip: Brush a small amount of oil on grater before shredding cheese for easier cleaning.

33

HAMBURGER STROGANOFF

1 pound ground beef
3 slices bacon, diced
1 medium onion, chopped
1 (10¾-ounce) can cream of mushroom soup,
    undiluted
¼ teaspoon paprika
1 (8-ounce) carton commercial sour cream
1 (8-ounce) package wide egg noodles

Cook ground beef, bacon, and onion in a
large skillet over medium heat until meat is
browned and onion is tender; stir to crumble
meat. Drain; reduce heat to low. Stir in soup
and paprika. Cook, uncovered, 20 minutes, stirring frequently. Stir in sour cream, and heat
through; do not boil.

Cook noodles according to package direc-
tions; drain. Spoon stroganoff over hot noodles.
Yield: 4 servings.   *Adell Kneifel,*
Yorktown, Tex.

LASAGNA

1 pound ground beef
1 clove garlic, crushed
1 tablespoon dried parsley flakes
2 teaspoons salt, divided
1 (28-ounce) can whole tomatoes, quartered
    and undrained
1 (12-ounce) can tomato paste
12 lasagna noodles
1 (12-ounce) carton cottage cheese
2 eggs, beaten
½ teaspoon pepper
½ cup grated Parmesan cheese
4 cups (16 ounces) shredded mozzarella
    cheese

Cook ground beef in a large skillet over
medium heat until browned, stirring to crumble; drain. Stir in garlic, parsley, 1 teaspoon
salt, tomatoes, and tomato paste. Simmer, uncovered, 45 minutes or until thickened; set aside.

Cook noodles according to package directions; drain.

Combine cottage cheese, eggs, 1 teaspoon
salt, pepper, and Parmesan cheese; mix well.
Layer half of noodles, cottage cheese mixture,
mozzarella, and meat sauce in a greased 13- x 9-
x 2-inch baking dish. Repeat layers; bake at
375° for 30 minutes. Yield: 6 to 8 servings.
Jacqueline M. Jones,
Hamburg, La.

EASY SPAGHETTI DINNER

2 pounds ground beef
3 cups chopped onion
2 green peppers, chopped
1 (28-ounce) can whole tomatoes, undrained
1 (12-ounce) can tomato paste
1 (15-ounce) can tomato sauce
3 tablespoons Worcestershire sauce
1 teaspoon chili powder
1 (12-ounce) package thin spaghetti
Grated Parmesan cheese (optional)
Chopped parsley (optional)

Cook ground beef in a Dutch oven over
medium heat until browned, stirring to crumble
meat; drain well. Add onion and green pepper;
cook until tender. Stir in tomatoes, tomato
paste, tomato sauce, Worcestershire sauce, and
chili powder. Simmer, uncovered, 2 hours, stirring occasionally.

Cook spaghetti according to package directions; drain. Serve sauce over spaghetti. Top
with Parmesan cheese and parsley, if desired.
Yield: 8 servings.   *Mrs. Ralph Jeffreys,*
Town Creek, Ala.

DELICIOUS BEEF ROAST

1 (1⅜-ounce) envelope dry onion soup mix
1 (10¾-ounce) can cream of mushroom soup,
    undiluted
1⅓ cups water
½ teaspoon pepper
1 (5- to 6-pound) chuck, sirloin tip, or
    shoulder roast
5 medium potatoes, peeled and halved
5 carrots, peeled and cut into 2-inch pieces

Combine soup mix, mushroom soup, water and pepper. Place roast in a Dutch oven; add soup mixture. Bring to a boil; cover, reduce heat, and simmer 2 hours. Add vegetables; cook 45 minutes. Yield: 10 to 12 servings.

Pauline Lester,
Saluda, S.C.

BEEF WELLINGTON

1 (3-pound) boneless eye of round beef roast
1 tablespoon meat tenderizer
3 tablespoons butter or margarine, melted
1 (8-ounce) package liverwurst spread
1 cup chopped fresh mushrooms
2 tablespoons bourbon
2 (10-ounce) packages frozen patty shells, thawed
1 egg yolk
1 tablespoon whipping cream

Moisten roast with water; sprinkle meat tenderizer on all sides of roast and pierce with a fork. Brown roast on all sides in butter in a large skillet; set aside.

Combine liverwurst spread, mushrooms, and bourbon; beat until smooth and set aside.

On a lightly floured surface, gently press edges of patty shells together. Roll into a ⅛-inch-thick rectangle. Spread one-third of liverwurst mixture on top of roast. Place roast lengthwise in middle of pastry, top side down. Spread remaining liverwurst mixture over sides of roast. Bring sides of pastry up to overlap on underside of roast; overlap slightly to form a seam, trimming off excess pastry. Trim ends of pastry to make even; fold over ends of pastry to seal.

Combine egg yolk and whipping cream; brush evenly over pastry. Roll out pastry trimmings; cut into decorative shapes and arrange on top of pastry, as desired. Brush shapes with remaining yolk mixture. Bake in a lightly greased 13- x 9- x 2-inch baking pan at 425° for 1 hour. Transfer to serving platter. Let roast stand 10 minutes before slicing. Yield: 8 to 10 servings.

Laurie C. Beppler,
Norfolk, Va.

WESTERN POT ROAST

1 (3-pound) beef brisket or chuck roast
1 tablespoon vegetable oil
1 cup chopped onion
1 cup catsup
¼ cup Worcestershire sauce
2 tablespoons brown sugar
2 tablespoons cider vinegar
1½ teaspoons salt

Brown beef in hot oil in a Dutch oven; remove and set aside.

Sauté onion in pan drippings until golden. Return beef to Dutch oven. Combine remaining ingredients; pour over meat. Cover and simmer 2½ to 3 hours or until meat is tender. Yield: 8 to 10 servings.

Janice Finn,
Greensburg, Ky.

BEEF-CARROT ROLLS

1½ pounds boneless round steak
¼ cup all-purpose flour
½ teaspoon salt
¼ teaspoon pepper
4 to 5 small carrots, peeled and cut into strips
2 tablespoons vegetable oil
1 (10¾-ounce) can cream of mushroom soup, diluted
4 medium potatoes, quartered
4 small onions, quartered

Trim excess fat from steak. Pound to ½ inch thick; cut into 4 pieces.

Combine flour, salt, and pepper. Dredge steak pieces in flour mixture. Place one-fourth of carrot sticks on each steak piece. Roll up each piece jellyroll fashion; secure with a wooden pick. Brown steak rolls in hot oil in a large skillet. Add diluted soup; cover, and cook over low heat 35 minutes. Add vegetables; cover, and continue to cook 25 minutes or until vegetables are tender. Yield: 4 servings.

Mrs. J. W. Hopkins,
Abilene, Tex.

STEAK ROLL-UPS

½ cup uncooked regular rice
¼ teaspoon ground thyme
½ teaspoon ground marjoram
¼ cup sliced green onion
¼ cup chopped pimiento
1 (4-ounce) can chopped mushrooms, undrained
2 tablespoons butter or margarine, melted
2 pounds boneless round steak
2 tablespoons shortening
¼ cup dry onion soup mix
1 cup water
½ cup cold water
2 tablespoons all-purpose flour

Cook rice according to package directions. Add thyme, marjoram, green onion, pimiento, mushrooms, and butter. Set aside.

Place meat on a piece of waxed paper and pound with a meat mallet until flattened to a thickness of ¼ inch. Cut into 6 pieces. Spread with rice mixture. Roll up and fasten with wooden picks. Brown in hot shortening; pour off drippings. Add soup mix and 1 cup water. Cover and simmer 1½ hours or until tender. Remove meat to a warm platter.

Gradually add ½ cup cold water to flour, stirring constantly. Stir into soup mixture; cook until thickened. Serve gravy over steak rolls. Yield: 6 servings.   *Mrs. Herbert Hill,*
Iuka, Miss.

OVEN SWISS STEAK

¼ cup all-purpose flour
1 teaspoon salt
1½ pounds boneless round steak, ½ inch thick
3 tablespoons vegetable oil
1 (16-ounce) can stewed tomatoes, undrained
½ cup chopped celery
½ cup peeled and chopped carrot
2 tablespoons chopped onion
½ teaspoon Worcestershire sauce
¼ cup (1 ounce) shredded process American cheese

Combine flour and salt. Sprinkle 1 tablespoon flour mixture on meat; pound into meat. Turn meat and repeat process. Reserve remaining flour mixture.

Cut meat into serving-size pieces. Heat oil in a large skillet; brown meat on both sides. Remove meat and place in a shallow baking dish.

Blend remaining flour with pan drippings. Add remaining ingredients except cheese; cook, stirring constantly, until mixture boils. Pour over meat; cover and bake at 350° about 1 hour or until meat and vegetables are tender. Sprinkle cheese over meat and return to oven for 5 minutes or until cheese is melted. Yield: 4 to 6 servings.   *Kim Riggleman,*
Reedsville, W. Va.

CHINESE-STYLE PEPPER STEAK

2 pounds boneless top round steak
¼ cup vegetable oil
3 medium-size green peppers, coarsley chopped
1 cup thinly sliced celery
½ cup diced onion
2 cloves garlic, minced
1 cup beef broth
1 teaspoon salt
¼ teaspoon pepper
¼ cup soy sauce
¼ cup water
2 tablespoons cornstarch
Hot cooked rice

Partially freeze steak; slice across the grain into 3- x ⅛-inch strips. Brown steak in hot oil in a large skillet; add next 7 ingredients. Cover, reduce heat, and simmer 15 minutes.

Combine soy sauce, water, and cornstarch; stir well. Add to meat mixture; cook, stirring constantly, until thickened. Serve over rice. Yield: 8 servings.   *Peggy Hancock,*
Teague, Tex.

Tip: Use baking soda on a damp cloth to shine up your kitchen appliances.

HONEY-ORANGE GLAZED HAM

1 (5- to 7-pound) uncooked ham
1 (6-ounce) can frozen orange juice
    concentrate, thawed and undiluted
1¾ cups water
¾ cup honey
1½ tablespoons cornstarch

Place ham, fat side up, in a 13- x 9- x 2-inch baking pan; set aside. Combine orange juice concentrate, water, honey, and cornstarch in a medium saucepan, stirring well. Cook over medium heat until thickened, stirring constantly. Pour half of glaze mixture over ham; bake, uncovered, at 325° for 2 to 2¾ hours (22 to 25 minutes per pound).

Remove ham from oven about 30 minutes before it is done. Score ham in a diamond pattern, making cuts ¼ inch deep in ham fat. Spoon remaining glaze mixture over ham, and return ham to oven. Bake, uncovered, for 30 minutes, basting frequently. Yield: 10 to 12 servings.
Mrs. Parke Cory,
Neosho, Mo.

HAM BALLS WITH SPICED CHERRY SAUCE

2 cups ground cooked ham
⅓ cup dry breadcrumbs
¼ cup milk
1 egg, beaten
⅛ teaspoon pepper
¼ cup vegetable oil
¼ cup hot water
1 cup cherry preserves
2½ tablespoons lemon juice
¾ teaspoon ground cinnamon
¼ teaspoon ground cloves

Combine ham, breadcrumbs, milk, egg, and pepper; mix well. Shape into 1½-inch balls. Heat vegetable oil in a skillet over medium heat; add ham balls and cook until browned on all sides. Pour off drippings and add hot water

to skillet. Cover pan and simmer ham balls 15 to 20 minutes.

Combine cherry preserves, lemon juice, cinnamon, and cloves in a small saucepan. Cook over low heat until mixture comes to a boil, stirring occasionally.

Place ham balls in a chafing dish or on a warm platter and spoon on sauce. Yield: 4 to 6 servings.
Mrs. A. Stancill,
Bel Air, Md.

SWEET-AND-SOUR PORK

1 (20-ounce) can pineapple chunks
1½ pounds boneless pork shoulder, cut into
    2½- x 2½-inch pieces
3 tablespoons vegetable oil
½ cup water
¼ cup firmly packed light brown sugar
2 tablespoons cornstarch
½ teaspoon salt
¼ cup cider vinegar
2 tablespoons soy sauce
1 small green pepper, cut into strips
1 small onion, thinly sliced
Hot cooked rice

Drain pineapple, reserving juice; set aside.
Brown pork in oil in a large skillet; stir in ½ cup water. Cover and simmer 1 hour or until tender. Combine sugar, cornstarch, and salt in a medium bowl; stir in reserved pineapple juice, vinegar, and soy sauce. Add to pork and cook, stirring constantly, until smooth and thickened. Add pineapple, green pepper, and onion; toss lightly and cook an additional 2 to 3 minutes. Serve over rice. Yield: 4 to 6 servings.
Dorothy L. Anderson,
Manor, Tex.

PORK CHOPS JARDINIERE

4 (½-inch-thick) pork chops
1 tablespoon vegetable oil
2 chicken-flavored bouillon cubes
1½ cups boiling water
1 teaspoon salt
½ teaspoon pepper
½ teaspoon sugar
2 stalks celery, chopped
1 carrot, peeled and chopped
1 tablespoon all-purpose flour
Mashed potatoes (optional)

Brown pork chops on both sides in hot oil in a large skillet; drain pan drippings.

Dissolve bouillon cubes in boiling water; pour over pork chops. Stir in remaining ingredients, except mashed potatoes. Bring to a boil; cover and simmer about 1 hour or until tender. Serve pork chops over mashed potatoes, if desired. Yield: 4 servings.   *Alda Reynolds,*
Lincolnton, N.C.

SWEET-AND-SOUR PORK CHOPS

4 lean pork chops
Salt
All-purpose flour
2 tablespoons vegetable oil
1 (13¼-ounce) can pineapple chunks, drained
1 small green pepper, cut into rings
1 cup chicken broth
1 cup sugar
1 cup vinegar
⅓ cup catsup
2 tablespoons cornstarch
¼ cup water
Hot cooked rice

Sprinkle pork chops with salt and dredge in flour; brown on both sides in hot oil. Place chops in a shallow 10-inch casserole. Top with pineapple and green pepper.

Combine next 4 ingredients in a small saucepan; bring to a boil. Reduce heat to medium. Combine cornstarch and water; stir well. Add cornstarch mixture to chicken broth mixture; stir constantly until thickened and bubbly. Pour chicken broth mixture over chops. Cover and bake at 325° for 1 hour or until done. Serve over rice. Yield: 4 servings.

Note: 1 chicken-flavored bouillon cube dissolved in 1 cup water may be substituted for 1 cup chicken broth.   *Zelda Dawson,*
Altus, Ark.

PORK CHOPS IN MUSHROOM SAUCE

1 cup all-purpose flour
½ teaspoon salt
½ teaspoon dried whole oregano
½ teaspoon pepper
6 pork chops
¼ cup vegetable oil
1 (10¾-ounce) can cream of mushroom soup, undiluted
1 (4-ounce) can sliced mushrooms, undrained
Hot cooked rice

Combine flour, salt, oregano, and pepper; blend well. Coat pork chops with flour mixture; brown on both sides in hot oil in a large skillet. Add soup and mushrooms; cover and simmer 40 minutes or until done. Serve with rice. Yield: 6 servings.   *Rosemary Jones,*
Mansfield, La.

TANGY BARBECUED RIBS

¼ cup chopped onion
2 tablespoons vegetable oil
1 cup chili sauce
½ cup tomato juice
¼ cup lemon juice
¼ cup firmly packed brown sugar
2 tablespoons Worcestershire sauce
6 drops hot sauce
3 pounds back or country-style pork ribs
Salt and pepper

Sauté onion in hot oil in a small saucepan until tender. Add next 6 ingredients; simmer 20 minutes.

Cut ribs into serving-size pieces; season with salt and pepper. Place ribs on grill, 5 inches from heat, over slow coals. Grill 45 minutes to 1 hour or until done, turning frequently. Brush ribs with sauce during last 20 minutes. Serve remaining sauce over ribs. Yield: 4 servings.

Mrs. S. R. Griffith,
Memphis, Tenn.

PORK CHALUPAS

1 (1-pound) package dried pinto beans
1 (3-pound) pork loin roast
1 (4-ounce) can green chiles
2 tablespoons cumin seeds
1 tablespoon salt
2 cloves garlic, chopped
1 teaspoon dried oregano leaves
Corn chips
Shredded Cheddar cheese
Shredded lettuce
Chopped onion
Diced tomato
1 (7½-ounce) jar jalapeño relish

Sort beans and wash thoroughly. Combine beans, roast, chiles, cumin seeds, salt, garlic, and oregano in a large Dutch oven; cover with water. Cover and simmer 6 hours, stirring occasionally; add water as needed.

Remove roast from Dutch oven; cut meat from bone, and break meat apart. Return meat to Dutch oven. Cook, uncovered, 1 to 1½ hours or until mixture is thickened.

To serve, place corn chips on individual serving plates. Top each with meat mixture, cheese, lettuce, onion, and tomato. Serve with jalapeño relish. Yield: 8 to 10 servings.

Mrs. Gary Denson,
Lineville, Ala.

Tip: Keep bacon drippings in a coffee can in the refrigerator and use for browning meats or in a hot salad dressing.

PORK LOAF

2 pounds lean ground pork
¼ cup catsup
1 egg, slightly beaten
1 cup cracker crumbs
1½ teaspoons salt
½ teaspoon pepper
3 tablespoons catsup

Combine all ingredients except 3 tablespoons catsup in a large bowl; mix well. Press firmly into a 9- x 5- x 3-inch loafpan. Spread 3 tablespoons catsup over top. Bake at 350° about 1 hour or until done. Yield: 6 to 8 servings.

Mrs. Allen Franks,
Guthrie, Ky.

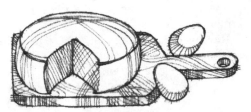

CHEESE GRITS AND SAUSAGE

2 (12-ounce) packages small link sausage
1 cup quick-cooking grits, uncooked
4 cups boiling water
1 teaspoon salt
½ cup butter or margarine
1 (6-ounce) roll process cheese food with garlic
2 eggs, beaten

Partially cook sausage; drain and set aside.

Stir grits into boiling water; add salt. Return to a boil; reduce heat and cook 2½ to 5 minutes, stirring frequently, until grits are thickened. Remove from heat. Add butter and cheese, stirring until melted.

Gradually stir about one-fourth of hot grits mixture into eggs; add eggs to remaining hot mixture, stirring constantly. Pour into a buttered 12- x 8- x 2-inch baking dish; arrange sausage links on top. Bake at 350° for 30 minutes. Yield: 8 to 10 servings.   *E. W. Pitzer,*
Bartlesville, Okla.

FRIED GRITS AND SAUSAGE

1 pound bulk sausage
1 cup quick-cooking grits, uncooked
4 cups boiling water
1 teaspoon salt
½ cup cornmeal
⅛ teaspoon pepper
¼ cup butter or margarine

Cook sausage until browned, stirring often; drain well.

Stir grits into boiling water; add salt. Return to a boil; reduce heat and cook 2½ to 5 minutes, stirring frequently, until grits are thickened. Add cornmeal and pepper; stir well. Add sausage; mix well and pour into a greased 9- x 5- x 3-inch loafpan. Chill 8 to 10 hours or overnight.

Remove from pan; cut into 1-inch-thick slices. Melt butter in a skillet; brown slices on both sides. Yield: 8 servings.

Peggy Fowler Revels,
Woodruff, S.C.

BRUNCH CASSEROLE

1 pound bulk sausage
1 (8-ounce) can refrigerated crescent
    dinner rolls
2 cups (8 ounces) shredded mozzarella cheese
4 eggs, beaten
¾ cup milk
¼ teaspoon salt
⅛ teaspoon pepper

Crumble sausage in a medium skillet; cook over medium heat until browned, stirring occasionally. Drain well. Line bottom of a buttered 13- x 9- x 2-inch baking dish with crescent rolls, firmly pressing perforations to seal. Sprinkle with sausage and cheese.

Combine remaining ingredients; beat well, and pour over sausage. Bake at 425° for 15 minutes or until set. Let stand 5 minutes; cut into squares and serve immediately. Yield: 6 to 8 servings.
Billie G. Costigan,
Mt. Sterling, Ky.

CHEESY SAUSAGE CASSEROLE

1½ pounds ground beef
1 pound hot bulk sausage
1 large onion, chopped
1 large green pepper, chopped
Salt and pepper to taste
1 hot pepper, chopped (optional)
1 (17-ounce) can cream-style corn
1 (15-ounce) can chili with beans
3 tablespoons chili powder
2 (8-ounce) cans tomato sauce
2 cups (8 ounces) shredded Cheddar cheese
1 (12-ounce) package wide egg noodles,
    cooked and drained

Crumble ground beef and sausage in a large skillet; add onion, green pepper, salt, pepper, and hot pepper, if desired. Cook over medium heat until meat is browned and onion is tender. Drain well. Stir in remaining ingredients, mixing well. Spoon into a lightly greased 3-quart casserole. Bake at 350° for 25 to 30 minutes or until bubbly. Yield: 12 servings.

Gayle Hurdle,
Carthage, Miss.

SAUSAGE AND NOODLE CASSEROLE

1 pound bulk sausage
½ cup chopped onion
¼ cup chopped green pepper
1 (10¾-ounce) can cream of chicken soup,
    undiluted
1⅓ cups water
1 (8-ounce) package egg noodles, cooked and
    drained
Salt and pepper to taste
½ cup canned French-fried onion rings,
    crushed

Crumble sausage in a large skillet; add onion and green pepper. Cook over medium heat until meat is browned and vegetables are tender, stirring occasionally. Drain well.

Combine soup and water; stir into meat mixture. Add noodles, salt, and pepper; mix well. Spoon mixture into a greased 2-quart casserole. Sprinkle with crushed onion rings. Bake at 350° for 30 minutes or until bubbly. Yield: 4 to 6 servings.

Mrs. Max E. Ayer,
Elizabethton, Tenn.

SAUSAGE MANICOTTI

1 pound Italian link sausage
¼ cup water
1 medium onion, chopped
1 pound ground beef
3 (10½-ounce) cans tomato puree
1 (6-ounce) can tomato paste
1¾ teaspoons dried whole basil, divided
1½ teaspoons salt, divided
1 teaspoon sugar
½ teaspoon pepper
1 cup water
1 (8-ounce) package manicotti shells
2 (16-ounce) cartons cottage cheese
1 (8-ounce) package mozzarella cheese, diced
2 eggs, slightly beaten
2 tablespoons chopped parsley
Grated Parmesan cheese

Place sausage and ¼ cup water in a heavy skillet; cover and cook 5 minutes. Uncover and brown sausage well; drain on paper towels, discard drippings, and set sausage aside.

Brown onion and ground beef in skillet. Stir in tomato puree, tomato paste, 1 teaspoon basil, 1 teaspoon salt, sugar, pepper, and 1 cup water; cover and simmer 45 minutes. Cut sausage links into bite-size pieces and add to sauce; cook 15 minutes, stirring occasionally.

Cook manicotti shells according to package directions. Combine cottage cheese and mozzarella cheese, eggs, ¾ teaspoon basil, ½ teaspoon salt, and parsley; stuff mixture into manicotti shells.

Spoon half of sauce into a 13- x 9- x 2-inch baking dish. Arrange stuffed shells over sauce. Spoon remaining sauce over shells. Sprinkle with Parmesan cheese. Bake at 375° for 1 hour; uncover and bake 15 additional minutes. Yield: 8 servings.

SAUSAGE SPAGHETTI

1 pound bulk sausage
1 cup chopped onion
½ cup chopped green pepper
½ teaspoon salt
½ to 1 teaspoon pepper
¼ teaspoon garlic powder
⅛ teaspoon chili powder
⅛ teaspoon ground thyme
1½ cups tomato juice
1 (8-ounce) can tomato sauce
1 teaspoon Worcestershire sauce
2 teaspoons vinegar
Dash of red pepper
1 (8-ounce) package spaghetti
½ cup grated Parmesan cheese

Crumble sausage in a Dutch oven; cook over medium heat until browned, stirring frequently. Add next 7 ingredients; cook 5 minutes, stirring frequently. Drain. Stir in next 5 ingredients; cover and simmer 10 minutes.

Cook spaghetti according to package directions; drain. Add spaghetti to meat sauce, mixing well. Remove to serving platter and sprinkle with Parmesan cheese. Yield: 6 to 8 servings.

Bonnie S. Baumgardner,
Sylva, N.C.

SAUSAGE CASSEROLE

1 large onion, finely chopped
1 pound bulk sausage
1 (4-ounce) package (2 envelopes) chicken
  noodle soup mix
½ cup uncooked regular rice
4½ cups water
1 (4-ounce) package slivered almonds
  (optional)

Brown onion and sausage in a large skillet, stirring to crumble sausage; drain. Add soup mix, rice, water, and almonds, if desired; mix well. Bring to a boil and simmer 7 minutes. Spoon into a greased 2½-quart casserole; bake at 400° for 30 minutes. Yield: 6 servings.

Joan Prescott,
Savannah, Ga.

MINTED CHICKEN

1 (2½- to 3-pound) broiler-fryer
Butter or margarine
Salt and pepper
1 cup plus 1 tablespoon fresh mint, divided
Commercial mint sauce (optional)

Rub outside of chicken lightly with butter. Sprinkle chicken inside and outside with salt and pepper. Place 1 cup fresh mint in cavity of chicken.

Place chicken, breast side up, on a rack in a shallow roasting pan. Bake at 375°, basting occasionally, for 1 hour and 15 minutes or until done. Sprinkle 1 tablespoon mint over chicken during last 10 minutes of baking. Serve with mint sauce, if desired. Yield: 4 to 6 servings.

Dale H. Hollabaugh,
Constantine, Ky.

BARBECUED CHICKEN

1 (2- to 3-pound) broiler-fryer, cut up
1 cup tomato juice
1 tablespoon plus 1 teaspoon cornstarch
2 tablespoons brown sugar
2 tablespoons Worcestershire sauce
1½ tablespoons vinegar
½ teaspoon salt
¼ teaspoon pepper
¼ teaspoon ground cinnamon
Dash of ground cloves

Place chicken in a shallow pan. Combine tomato juice and cornstarch; stir well. Add sugar, Worcestershire sauce, vinegar, and seasonings to tomato juice mixture; stir well. Pour marinade over chicken; cover and refrigerate 1 to 2 hours, turning chicken at least once.

Remove chicken from marinade, reserving marinade. Place chicken, skin side down, on grill. Cover with aluminum foil. Grill chicken over medium heat 45 to 60 minutes, turning and basting with marinade every 15 minutes. (Keep chicken covered with foil while grilling.) Yield: 4 servings.

Jeri Holcomb,
Boaz, Ala.

BAKED PARMESAN CHICKEN

1 egg, beaten
1 tablespoon milk
½ cup grated Parmesan cheese
¼ cup all-purpose flour
1 teaspoon paprika
½ teaspoon salt
Dash of pepper
1 (2½- to 3-pound) broiler-fryer, cut up and
  skinned
¼ cup butter or margarine, melted

Combine egg and milk; stir well and set aside. Combine Parmesan cheese, flour, paprika, salt, and pepper; mix well.

Rinse chicken, and pat dry. Dip in egg mixture; dredge in flour mixture. Place chicken in a 12- x 8- x 2-inch baking dish; pour butter over chicken. Bake at 350° for 1 hour or until tender. Yield: 4 servings.

Mrs. Alfred L. Stancill,
Bel Air, Md.

Tip: Lower oven temperature 25° when using heat-proof glass dishes to ensure even baking.

IMPERIAL CHICKEN

½ cup plus 2 tablespoons butter or
  margarine, melted
1 small clove garlic, crushed
¾ cup dry breadcrumbs
½ cup grated Parmesan cheese
1½ tablespoons minced parsley
1 teaspoon salt
Pepper to taste
3 whole chicken breasts, split, boned, and
  skinned
Juice of 1 lemon
Paprika

Combine butter and garlic; set aside. Combine breadcrumbs, Parmesan cheese, parsley, salt, and pepper; stir to blend. Dip each chicken breast in butter mixture and coat with breadcrumb mixture; roll tightly, starting at narrow end, and secure with a wooden pick.

Arrange chicken in a shallow baking pan. Drizzle with remaining butter mixture and lemon juice. Sprinkle with paprika. Bake at 350° for 45 to 55 minutes. Yield: 6 servings.

Mrs. Dale Taylor,
Beaverdam, Va.

GOLDEN OVEN-FRIED CHICKEN

¼ cup butter or margarine, divided
½ cup all-purpose flour
1 teaspoon salt
1 teaspoon dry mustard
1 teaspoon paprika
1 teaspoon pepper
1 (2½- to 3-pound) broiler-fryer, cut up

Melt 2 tablespoons butter in a 13- x 9- x 2-inch baking pan.

Combine next 5 ingredients; stir well. Dredge chicken in flour mixture, coating well. Place chicken in baking pan, and dot with remaining butter. Bake at 350° for 1 hour. Yield: 4 servings.

Charles Andrew,
Lynch Station, Va.

OVEN-FRIED CHICKEN PARMESAN

1 egg, beaten
1 tablespoon milk
½ cup all-purpose flour
¼ cup grated Parmesan cheese
1 teaspoon paprika
½ teaspoon salt
1 (2½- to 3-pound) broiler-fryer, cut up
¼ cup butter or margarine, melted

Combine egg and milk; stir well. Combine flour, Parmesan cheese, paprika, and salt, stirring well.

Dip each piece of chicken in egg mixture; dredge in flour mixture, coating well. Place chicken in a 13- x 9- x 2-inch baking dish. Drizzle butter over chicken. Bake at 350° for 1 hour or until done. Yield: 4 servings.

Janet Eubanks,
Paris, Ark.

COUNTRY FRIED CHICKEN

½ cup milk
1 egg, beaten
1 cup all-purpose flour
2 teaspoons garlic salt
1 teaspoon paprika
1 teaspoon pepper
¼ teaspoon poultry seasoning
1 (2½- to 3-pound) broiler-fryer, cut up
Vegetable oil

Combine milk and egg; stir well. Combine flour and seasonings, stirring well.

Dredge each piece of chicken in flour mixture; dip in milk mixture. Dredge again in flour mixture.

Heat ¾ inch of oil in a skillet to 365°; add chicken and cook until brown. Reduce heat to 275°; cook, uncovered, 25 to 30 minutes, turning occasionally. Drain on paper towels. Yield: 4 servings.

Gladys Hester,
Winston-Salem, N.C.

SKILLET FRIED CHICKEN

¾ cup buttermilk
1 teaspoon salt
¼ teaspoon pepper
1 (2- to 3-pound) broiler-fryer, cut up
1 cup all-purpose flour
1½ cups vegetable oil

Combine buttermilk, salt, and pepper; stir well. Place chicken in a shallow pan, and pour buttermilk mixture over top. Cover, and let stand 20 minutes, turning once. Remove chicken and drain.

Dredge chicken in flour, coating well. Heat oil in an electric skillet to 350°; add chicken and cook until browned, turning occasionally. Reduce heat to 275°; cover and cook 25 minutes. Uncover, and cook 5 additional minutes. Drain on paper towels. Yield: 4 servings.

Cora B. Patterson,
TyTy, Ga.

TURKEY-SPAGHETTI CASSEROLE

5 ounces spaghetti, broken into 2-inch pieces (1¼ cups)
1½ cups cubed cooked turkey
½ cup chopped onion
½ cup water
¼ cup chopped green pepper
¼ cup chopped pimiento
1 (10¾-ounce) can cream of mushroom soup, undiluted
¼ teaspoon salt
¼ to ½ teaspoon pepper
1¾ cups (7 ounces) shredded Cheddar cheese

Cook spaghetti according to package directions: drain and rinse.

Combine spaghetti and remaining ingredients in a large mixing bowl; mix well. Spoon into a greased, shallow 2-quart baking dish; bake at 350° for 45 minutes. Yield: about 6 servings.

Pearl Bradley,
Lampasas, Tex.

CRISPY TURKEY BAKE

3 cups cubed cooked turkey
1 (10-ounce) package frozen English peas, cooked and drained
1 cup (4 ounces) shredded sharp Cheddar cheese, divided
¼ cup chopped onion
½ teaspoon salt
Dash of pepper
½ cup mayonnaise
6 slices tomato
¾ cup crushed potato chips

Combine turkey, peas, ½ cup cheese, onion, salt, pepper, and mayonnaise; mix well. Spoon into a greased 10- x 6- x 2-inch baking dish; place tomato slices on top. Bake at 350° for 25 minutes. Combine remaining ½ cup cheese and potato chips; mix well, and sprinkle over casserole. Bake an additional 5 minutes or until cheese melts. Yield: 6 servings.

Charlotte A. Pierce,
Greensburg, Ky.

FRUIT-STUFFED GOOSE

1 (9- to 10-pound) dressed goose
3½ cups soft breadcrumbs
1½ cups peeled and chopped cooking apples
½ cup raisins
½ cup chopped onion
½ cup butter or margarine, melted
2 teaspoons salt
1 teaspoon ground sage
1 teaspoon dried whole rosemary
⅛ teaspoon pepper
Parsley (optional)
Grapes (optional)
Apples (optional)
Oranges (optional)

Remove giblets and neck from goose; reserve for giblet gravy, if desired. Rinse goose thoroughly with water; pat dry.

Combine next 9 ingredients, stirring well. Spoon dressing into cavity of goose; close with skewers. Truss goose, and place it, breast side up, on a rack in roasting pan. Bake, uncovered, at 350° for 4 hours or until meat thermometer registers 185° and drumsticks move easily. Baste occasionally with pan drippings.

Place goose on serving platter; garnish with parsley, grapes, apples, and oranges, if desired. Yield: 5 to 7 servings.   *Mrs. J. C. Graham,*
Athens, Tex.

BREAM IN PUFFY BEER BATTER

6 to 8 medium bream or crappie, cleaned and dressed
Lemon juice
2 cups all-purpose flour, divided
1 tablespoon plus 1 teaspoon salt, divided
1 tablespoon paprika
1 (12-ounce) can beer
Vegetable oil
Fresh parsley sprigs or watercress
Lemon wedges

Dry fish thoroughly; sprinkle lemon juice over both sides and allow to stand 15 minutes.

Combine 1 cup flour and 1 teaspoon salt; set aside. Combine 1 cup flour, 1 tablespoon salt, and paprika; add beer, mixing well.

Dredge fish in dry flour mixture; dip into beer batter. Fry fish in ½ inch hot oil (360°) until golden brown on both sides. Drain on paper towels. Garnish with parsley and lemon wedges. Yield: 6 to 8 servings.

Note: Batter may be stored in refrigerator up to 4 days.

CRUNCHY POTATO FISH FRY

1 (2-ounce) envelope instant mashed potatoes
2 tablespoons sesame seeds
1 egg, slightly beaten
1 tablespoon lemon juice
1 teaspoon salt
⅛ teaspoon pepper
2 pounds fish fillets
¼ to ½ cup shortening

Combine instant mashed potato granules and sesame seeds, mixing well; set aside.

Combine egg, lemon juice, salt, and pepper; mix well. Dip fish in egg mixture; dredge in potato mixture.

Melt shortening in a large skillet over medium heat; fry fish in shortening until golden brown on both sides. Yield: 5 servings.

Woodie Lowe,
Middlesboro, Ky.

TROUT SUPREME

6 to 8 trout or other small fish fillets
½ cup buttermilk
1 teaspoon salt
½ teaspoon soda
¾ cup all-purpose flour
Vegetable oil

Rinse trout fillets, and pat dry.

Combine buttermilk, salt, and soda; mix well. Dip fillets in buttermilk mixture; dredge in flour. Fry fish in ¼ inch hot oil (360°) until golden brown on both sides. Drain on paper towels. Yield: 6 to 8 servings.   *Janis Moyer,*
Farmersville, Tex.

PAN-FRIED TROUT IN BUTTER

4 small trout, cleaned and dressed
Salt and pepper
2 tablespoons milk
All-purpose flour
¼ cup butter or margarine
Fresh parsley sprigs
Lemon wedges

Rinse and dry fish thoroughly. Sprinkle fish with salt and pepper, and dip into milk. Sprinkle each side of fish with flour.

Melt butter in a large skillet over medium heat. Fry fish in butter until golden brown on both sides. Garnish with parsley and lemon wedges. Yield: 4 servings.

Mrs. Jessie M. Sumlin,
Newnan, Ga.

FILLET OF SOLE WITH DILL SAUCE

1 cup all-purpose flour
½ teaspoon salt
¼ teaspoon pepper
1½ pounds fillet of sole
About ⅓ cup butter, melted
Lemon juice
Dill Sauce

Combine flour, salt, and pepper; mix well. Dredge fillets in seasoned flour; fry in butter over low heat until golden brown on both sides. Sprinkle with lemon juice, and serve with Dill Sauce. Yield: about 4 servings.

DILL SAUCE:

1 (8-ounce) carton commercial sour cream
2 tablespoons lemon juice
1 teaspoon Worcestershire sauce
1 teaspoon onion juice
2 tablespoons chopped fresh dillweed
½ teaspoon dry mustard
¼ teaspoon salt
¼ teaspoon white pepper

Combine all ingredients in a small mixing bowl; mix well and chill. Yield: about 1 cup.
Mrs. M. Benonus,
Heathsville, Va.

SAUCY MACKEREL SUPREME

2 (1½-pound) mackerel, cleaned and dressed
½ teaspoon salt
½ teaspoon pepper
1 (16-ounce) can tomatoes, undrained
1 medium-size green pepper, chopped
1 medium onion, chopped
1 cup chopped celery
¼ cup water
Hot cooked rice

Lay fish flat on a cutting board; cut in half lengthwise down center back of fish. Place skin side down in electric skillet. Sprinkle fish with salt and pepper.

Combine remaining ingredients except rice; spoon over fish. Cook on low heat (200°) for 20 to 25 minutes until fish flakes easily when tested with a fork. Serve over rice. Yield: 4 servings.
F. P. Pridgen,
Fayetteville, N.C.

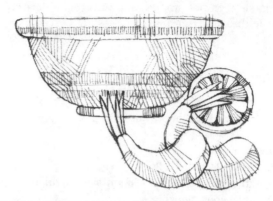

SHRIMP JAMBALAYA

¼ cup chopped onion
¼ cup chopped green pepper
¼ cup margarine, melted
3 tablespoons all-purpose flour
2 teaspoons chili powder
1 teaspoon salt
¼ teaspoon garlic powder
¼ teaspoon pepper
⅛ teaspoon red pepper
¼ cup Worcestershire sauce
1 tablespoon vinegar
2 cups chopped tomatoes
1 (10-ounce) package frozen sliced okra, broken into pieces
1½ pounds uncooked shrimp, peeled and deveined
2 cups hot cooked rice

Sauté onion and green pepper in margarine until tender. Combine flour and seasonings; blend into onion mixture. Stir in Worcestershire sauce and vinegar until smooth. Add tomatoes and okra, stirring constantly until thickened. Add shrimp and simmer uncovered for 15 minutes. Stir in rice. Yield: 6 to 8 servings.
Angela Thomas,
Goshen, Ala.

SANDWICH SOUFFLE

16 slices bread
Butter or margarine, softened
8 slices cooked ham or chicken
2 cups (8 ounces) shredded sharp Cheddar
   cheese
4 eggs, beaten
2 cups milk
1 teaspoon Dijon mustard
½ teaspoon Worcestershire sauce
Dash of salt
Dash of hot sauce

Trim crusts off bread. Spread butter on one side of each slice. Place 8 slices, buttered side down, in a 3-quart oblong baking dish. Place a ham slice on each piece of bread; sprinkle with half of cheese. Top with remaining bread slices to make 8 sandwiches. Sprinkle with remaining cheese.

Combine eggs, milk, mustard, Worcestershire sauce, salt, and hot sauce. Pour evenly over sandwiches. Cover; refrigerate overnight.

Remove dish from refrigerator, and allow to reach room temperature. Bake at 350° for 45 minutes to 1 hour. Yield: 8 servings.

Rosemary Bowers,
Seminole, Tex.

BUTTERMILK CHEESE SOUFFLE

¼ cup butter or margarine
¼ cup all-purpose flour
1 cup buttermilk
1 cup (4 ounces) shredded Cheddar cheese
1 teaspoon salt
1 teaspoon chopped parsley
⅛ teaspoon onion juice
Dash of red pepper
6 eggs, separated

Lightly butter a 1½-quart soufflé dish. Cut a piece of aluminum foil long enough to circle the dish, allowing a 1-inch overlap. Fold foil lengthwise into thirds, and lightly butter one side. Wrap foil, buttered side against the dish, so that it extends 3 inches above the rim. Attach foil securely with string.

Melt ¼ cup butter in a heavy saucepan over low heat; add flour, stirring until smooth. Cook 1 minute, stirring constantly. Gradually add buttermilk; cook over medium heat, stirring constantly, until thickened and bubbly. Stir in cheese, salt, parsley, onion juice, and red pepper.

Beat egg yolks. Gradually stir about one-fourth of hot mixture into yolks, stirring well; stir yolk mixture into hot mixture.

Beat egg whites (at room temperature) until stiff peaks form. Fold egg whites into cheese mixture. Spoon into prepared soufflé dish. Bake at 350° for 40 to 45 minutes. Remove collar before serving. Serve immediately. Yield: 8 servings.

Mary Fulcher,
Hobbs, N. Mex.

CHEESE OMELET

1 tablespoon all-purpose flour
½ cup milk
¼ teaspoon salt
4 eggs, slightly beaten
1 tablespoon butter, margarine, or
   vegetable oil
⅔ to 1 cup cubed Cheddar cheese

Combine flour, milk, and salt; mix until smooth. Stir into eggs. Melt butter in a 9- or 10-inch omelet pan or heavy skillet until just hot enough to sizzle a drop of water. Pour in egg mixture all at once.

Using a fork or spatula, lift cooked portions at the edges so that uncooked portions flow underneath. Move pan rapidly back and forth over heat to keep egg mixture in motion and sliding freely to avoid sticking. (When the mixture is set properly, it no longer flows freely and is moist and creamy on top.)

Sprinkle cheese over eggs; continue cooking 1 minute longer or until bottom is slightly browned. Fold in half or roll, turning out onto plate. Serve immediately. Yield: 2 servings.

Carolyn Beyer,
Fredericksburg, Tex.

RANCHER'S OMELET

6 slices bacon, diced
2 tablespoons finely chopped onion
1 cup grated raw potato
6 eggs, slightly beaten
½ teaspoon salt
⅛ teaspoon white pepper
Dash of hot sauce
2 tablespoons minced fresh parsley

Fry bacon until crisp; drain and set aside, reserving 2 tablespoons drippings in skillet. Sauté onion until soft in reserved drippings. Add potato and cook until light brown. Pour eggs into skillet. Add salt, pepper, and hot sauce. Cook over low heat, lifting up edges with spatula to let uncooked egg mixture flow underneath. When firm, sprinkle with crumbled bacon and parsley. Fold omelet in half; serve immediately. Yield: 4 to 6 servings.

Mildred Clute,
Marquez, Tex.

MAKE-AHEAD BREAKFAST BAKE

1 pound bulk sausage
2 slices bread, cut into ½-inch cubes
1 cup (4 ounces) shredded sharp Cheddar
   cheese
6 eggs
2 cups milk
½ teaspoon salt
½ teaspoon dry mustard

Crumble sausage in a medium skillet; cook over medium heat until browned, stirring occasionally. Drain well.

Spread bread cubes in a buttered 12- x 8- x 2-inch baking dish; top with sausage and cheese.

Combine eggs, milk, and seasonings; beat well, and pour over cheese. Cover and refrigerate overnight. Bake at 350° for 30 to 40 minutes or until set. Yield: 6 to 8 servings.

Mrs. Steven Terry,
Sand Springs, Okla.

TEXAS BRUNCH

3 tablespoons butter or margarine
3 tablespoons all-purpose flour
2 cups milk
¼ teaspoon salt
⅛ teaspoon pepper
6 hard-cooked eggs, peeled and chopped
½ cup mayonnaise or salad dressing
Buttermilk Cornbread (recipe follows)
Chopped green onion
Crumbled cooked bacon
Shredded Cheddar cheese

Melt butter in a heavy saucepan over low heat; add flour, stirring until smooth. Gradually stir in milk; cook until thickened and bubbly. Add salt, pepper, eggs, and mayonnaise, mixing well.

To serve, slice cornbread squares in half horizontally; spoon egg mixture over cornbread; garnish with onion, bacon, and cheese. Yield: 9 servings.

BUTTERMILK CORNBREAD:

1 cup yellow cornmeal
⅓ cup all-purpose flour
1 teaspoon baking powder
½ teaspoon salt
¼ teaspoon soda
1 egg, beaten
1 cup buttermilk

Combine dry ingredients; add egg and buttermilk, mixing well. Pour batter into a well-greased 8-inch square pan. Bake at 400° for 20 minutes or until lightly browned. Cut into squares. Yield: 9 servings.

Mrs. N. A. Gilcrease,
Corsicana, Tex.

The coating is light, crisp, and a beautiful golden brown on Bream in Puffy Beer Batter (page 45).

Overleaf: *Bring flavorful fruit to your holiday table in Honey Fruit Salad (page 52) or Festive Cranberry Salad (page 53).*

Salads

FRESH FRUIT SALAD

2 oranges, peeled and sectioned
2 apples, unpeeled and cubed
2 bananas, peeled and sliced
Salad Dressing (recipe follows)

Combine fruit. Serve with salad dressing. Yield: 4 to 6 servings.

SALAD DRESSING:

1 cup orange juice
½ cup sugar
2 teaspoons cornstarch

Combine all ingredients in a small saucepan. Cook, stirring constantly, until thickened. Cool. Yield: about 1 cup.

Mrs. Galen Johnson,
Transylvania, La.

FROZEN FRUIT SALAD

1 (8-ounce) carton frozen whipped topping, thawed
1 (8-ounce) carton commercial sour cream
1 (6-ounce) bottle maraschino cherries, drained and chopped
1 (15¼-ounce) can crushed pineapple, drained
5 bananas, peeled and mashed
1 cup chopped pecans

Combine all ingredients; mix well. Spoon into an 8-inch square dish; cover with foil and freeze. Move from freezer to refrigerator 30 to 45 minutes before serving. Cut into squares. Yield: 9 servings.
Dorothy Cox,
Snyder, Tex.

FROSTY FRUIT SALAD

1 (8-ounce) package Neufchâtel cheese, softened
1 (8-ounce) carton commercial sour cream
¼ cup sugar
¼ teaspoon salt
1 (17-ounce) can apricot halves, drained and halved
1 (16-ounce) can pitted dark sweet cherries, drained
1 (8-ounce) can crushed pineapple, drained
1 cup miniature marshmallows

Beat cheese until smooth; add sour cream, sugar, and salt, mixing well. Gently stir in fruit and marshmallows; spoon into a lightly oiled 5-cup mold. Freeze at least 6 hours or until firm. To serve, let salad stand at room temperature 5 to 10 minutes; cut into slices. Yield: 8 servings.
Mrs. Ben Caldwell,
Gay, Ga.

FRUIT MELANGE DELIGHT

1 large fresh pineapple
2 to 3 oranges
2 pears, peeled, cored, and diced
1 cup seedless grapes, halved
Ginger-Yogurt Dressing

Cut pineapple (including leafy top) in half lengthwise. Hollow out pineapple, leaving shell ½-inch thick. Remove core and cut pineapple into chunks. Reserve juice that collects when pineapple is being prepared.

Peel and section oranges, reserving juice. Combine pineapple juice and orange juice to make ¼ cup; set juice mixture aside for dressing.

Combine pineapple chunks, oranges, pears, and grapes; spoon into pineapple shells. Top with Ginger-Yogurt Dressing. Yield: about 6 servings.

GINGER-YOGURT DRESSING:

1 (8-ounce) carton plain yogurt
¼ cup reserved fruit juices
Ground ginger

Stir together yogurt and juice; add ginger to taste. Chill. Yield: about 1 cup.
Karen Cromer,
Anderson, S.C.

HONEY FRUIT SALAD

1 (15¼-ounce) can pineapple chunks,
  undrained
2 medium oranges, peeled and sectioned
1 large apple, diced
1 banana, peeled and sliced
½ cup chopped pecans
½ cup orange juice
¼ cup honey
1 tablespoon lemon juice

Combine first 5 ingredients in a large bowl; set aside. Combine remaining ingredients; pour over fruit mixture, stirring gently. Chill. Yield: 6 servings.
Mrs. Jack Poynor,
Fayetteville, Ark.

24-HOUR FRUIT SALAD

4 egg yolks, beaten
Juice of 1 lemon
½ cup milk
1 (16-ounce) package miniature marshmallows
1 pound seedless grapes
1 (29-ounce) can pineapple chunks, drained
1 cup chopped walnuts or pecans
1 cup whipping cream, whipped

Combine egg yolks, lemon juice, and milk in top of a double boiler; cook, stirring constantly, until thickened. Cool. Combine marshmallows, grapes, pineapple, walnuts, and cooked mixture, blending well. Chill overnight. Fold in whipped cream and chill. Yield: 12 to 15 servings.
Bird Helmick,
Vici, Okla.

BANANA-PEAR COMBO

2 tablespoons mayonnaise or salad dressing
2 tablespoons commercial sour cream
1 tablespoon lemon juice
1 teaspoon sugar or honey
⅛ teaspoon ground ginger
2 bananas, peeled and sliced
2 pears, unpeeled, cored, and diced
½ cup thinly sliced celery
¼ cup chopped walnuts
Lettuce leaves (optional)

Combine first 5 ingredients; mix well. Add remaining ingredients, except lettuce; toss lightly to coat. Serve in lettuce-lined bowls, if desired. Yield: 4 servings.
Marie Raney,
Dogpatch, Ark.

FROZEN CHERRY SALAD

1 (1.25-ounce) envelope whipped topping mix
1 (8-ounce) package cream cheese, softened
1 (20-ounce) can crushed pineapple, drained
1 (16½-ounce) can pitted dark sweet cherries,
  drained

Prepare topping mix according to package directions. Combine prepared topping and cream cheese; beat until smooth. Fold in fruits. Spoon into an 8-inch square dish; cover and freeze. Yield: 9 servings.   *Gail Smith,*
White Hall, Md.

FESTIVE CRANBERRY SALAD

4 cups fresh cranberries, ground
1 large orange, unpeeled, seeded, and ground
1 cup sugar
1 (3-ounce) package lemon-flavored gelatin
1 envelope unflavored gelatin
1 cup boiling water
1 (15-ounce) can crushed pineapple, undrained
1 cup chopped pecans
½ cup diced celery
Lettuce leaves

Combine ground cranberries, ground orange, and sugar; cover and chill 1 hour.

Dissolve gelatin in boiling water; gently stir in cranberry mixture, pineapple, pecans, and celery. Spoon mixture into a 5-cup mold; chill until firm. Unmold on a lettuce-lined serving plate. Yield: 8 servings.   *Mrs. Lewis Self,*
Sylvania, Ga.

FROSTED ORANGE SALAD

1 (6-ounce) package orange-flavored gelatin
1 envelope unflavored gelatin
1 cup boiling water
1 pint orange sherbet, softened
1 (20-ounce) can crushed pineapple, undrained
1 (11-ounce) can mandarin oranges, drained
½ cup orange juice
1 egg, beaten
½ cup sugar
1 tablespoon all-purpose flour
1 (1.25-ounce) envelope whipped topping mix

Dissolve gelatin in boiling water in a large bowl. Gently stir in sherbet, pineapple, and oranges. Pour mixture into a 12- x 8- x 2-inch dish; set aside.

Combine orange juice, egg, sugar, and flour in a small saucepan; cook over medium heat until thickened, stirring constantly. Cool.

Prepare topping mix according to package directions. Fold into cooked orange juice mixture; spread evenly over salad. Cover and chill overnight. Yield: 12 servings.
Barbara D. Walker,
Rocky Mount, N.C.

SURPRISE RASPBERRY SALAD

1 (16-ounce) can whole beets
1 (20-ounce) can crushed pineapple, undrained
Juice of 1 lemon
¼ cup vinegar
1 tablespoon sugar
¼ cup water
Dash of salt
1 (3-ounce) package raspberry-flavored gelatin
1 teaspoon unflavored gelatin
½ cup chopped pecans

Drain beets and pineapple, reserving liquids. Cut beets into julienne strips; set aside. Combine reserved liquids, lemon juice, vinegar, sugar, water, and salt. Bring to a boil; add raspberry and unflavored gelatin and stir to dissolve. Chill until consistency of unbeaten egg white. Fold in beets, pineapple, and pecans. Pour into a 6-cup mold; chill until firm. Yield: 8 to 10 servings.   *Florence L. Costello,*
Chattanooga, Tenn.

CARROT SALAD

1 (3-ounce) package orange-flavored gelatin
1 cup boiling water
1 cup cold water
2 cups peeled and grated carrots
1 (8-ounce) can crushed pineapple, drained
½ cup flaked coconut
¼ cup chopped pecans

Dissolve gelatin in boiling water; add cold water and chill until consistency of unbeaten egg white. Stir in remaining ingredients. Pour into a lightly greased 1-quart mold or individual molds. Chill until firm. Yield: 6 servings.
Carolyn Beyer,
Fredericksburg, Tex.

CARROT AMBROSIA

4 cups peeled and shredded carrots
¼ cup lemon juice
1 cup orange sections (about 3 oranges)
1 (3½-ounce) can flaked coconut
1½ cups miniature marshmallows
3 tablespoons honey
½ cup commercial sour cream
¼ cup mayonnaise
Lettuce leaves (optional)

Combine first 5 ingredients in a large bowl. Set aside. Combine honey, sour cream, and mayonnaise; mix well and pour over carrot mixture. Toss lightly. Chill. Serve on lettuce leaves, if desired. Yield: 8 to 10 servings.
Gladys C. Milton,
Valrico, Fla.

CORN SALAD

2 (12-ounce) cans shoe peg corn, drained
1 (10-ounce) jar pimiento-stuffed olives, drained and sliced
6 to 8 green onions, sliced
1 medium-size green pepper, finely chopped
1 cup commercial Italian dressing

Combine vegetables; add dressing and stir well. Cover; chill several hours or overnight. Yield: 6 to 8 servings. *Mrs. C. O. Story,*
Thibodaux, La.

CRISP COLESLAW

3 pounds cabbage, shredded
1 green pepper, chopped
1 red pepper, chopped
2 medium onions, chopped
2 cups sugar
1¼ cups vinegar
1 cup vegetable oil
1 tablespoon salt
2 teaspoons celery seeds

Combine cabbage, pepper, onion, and sugar in a large mixing bowl; mix well. Cover and chill 2 hours.
Combine vinegar, oil, salt, and celery seeds in a saucepan; bring to a boil, stirring until salt is dissolved. Pour over cabbage mixture; toss gently. Cover and chill at least 2 hours before serving. Coleslaw will keep for several days in the refrigerator. Yield: 18 to 20 servings.
Mary K. Owings,
Sentinel, Okla.

VEGETABLE SLAW

1 envelope unflavored gelatin
¼ cup cold water
⅔ cup sugar
⅔ cup vinegar
1 teaspoon celery seeds
1½ teaspoons salt
¼ teaspoon pepper
⅔ cup vegetable oil
8 cups shredded cabbage
2 carrots, peeled and shredded
1 green pepper, finely chopped
½ cup finely chopped onion

Soften gelatin in cold water; set aside. Combine sugar, vinegar, celery seeds, salt, and pepper in a small saucepan. Bring to a boil; stir in softened gelatin. Cool until slightly thickened. Beat well; gradually add oil, beating constantly. Refrigerate until needed.

Combine cabbage, carrot, green pepper, and onion; toss with dressing before serving. Yield: about 8 servings.

Mrs. Robert W. McNeil,
Ronceverte, W. Va.

SOUR CREAM POTATO SALAD

4 medium potatoes, cooked, peeled, and
    cubed
1 cup chopped celery
½ cup peeled and chopped cucumber
¼ cup chopped onion
1½ teaspoons salt
1 teaspoon celery seeds
¼ teaspoon pepper
1 (8-ounce) carton commercial sour cream
¼ to ½ cup mayonnaise
1 tablespoon prepared mustard
1 tablespoon vinegar
3 hard-cooked eggs

Combine first 7 ingredients; toss gently, and set aside.

Combine sour cream, mayonnaise, mustard, and vinegar; mix well. Slice eggs in half and remove yolks. Press yolks through a sieve; stir into sour cream mixture. Chop whites; gently stir into potato mixture. Add sour cream mixture to potato mixture; toss gently. Cover and chill 3 to 4 hours. Yield: 6 to 8 servings.

Floy Grindstaff,
Elizabethton, Tenn.

Tip: Remember that deep green, bright yellow, or orange fruits and vegetables are good sources of vitamin A. Good sources of vitamin C are citrus fruits, deep green vegetables, and potatoes.

RICE SALAD

3 cups cold cooked rice
½ cup sweet pickle relish
4 hard-cooked eggs, chopped
½ cup finely chopped onion
2 tablespoons chopped pimiento
1½ cups mayonnaise
Egg slices

Combine first 6 ingredients and toss. Chill thoroughly before serving. Garnish with egg slices. Yield: 6 to 8 servings.

Sue Berry,
DeWitt, Ark.

CHILLED STUFFED TOMATOES

6 large ripe tomatoes
Salt
⅓ cup finely chopped cucumber
⅓ cup grated onion
⅓ cup chopped green pepper
⅓ cup chopped celery
⅓ cup finely shredded cabbage
½ teaspoon salt
Dash of pepper
⅓ cup mayonnaise
Dash of hot sauce
Dash of curry powder
Lettuce leaves

Wash tomatoes; place in boiling water 1 minute. Drain and immediately plunge into cold water. Gently remove skins. With stem end up, cut each tomato into 4 wedges, cutting to, but not through, base of tomato. Spread wedges slightly apart. Sprinkle inside of shells with salt. Cover and chill 1½ hours.

Combine the next 7 ingredients; cover and chill.

To serve, spoon chilled filling into tomato shells. Combine mayonnaise, hot sauce, and curry powder. Top each tomato with a dollop of mayonnaise mixture. Serve on lettuce leaves. Yield: 6 servings.

Vegetable Salads   55

SAUERKRAUT SALAD

1 cup sugar
½ cup vegetable oil
½ cup vinegar
1 (27-ounce) can chopped sauerkraut, drained
1 cup diced green pepper
1 cup diced celery
1 onion, finely chopped

Combine sugar, oil, and vinegar in a small saucepan; bring to a boil and remove from heat. Combine vegetables; pour hot vinegar mixture over all. Cover and chill overnight. Yield: 8 to 10 servings. *Sue Berry, DeWitt, Ark.*

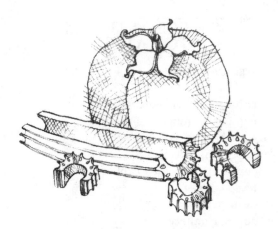

TOMATO BOWL

¼ cup chopped fresh parsley
¼ cup vegetable oil
2 tablespoons cider vinegar
2 teaspoons prepared mustard
1 teaspoon sugar
1 teaspoon salt
¼ teaspoon pepper
1 clove garlic, minced
6 firm, ripe, small tomatoes, sliced

Combine first 8 ingredients, mixing well. Place tomato slices in serving bowl, and add dressing. Cover and let stand at room temperature 20 minutes before serving. Yield: 8 to 10 servings.

TOMATO ASPIC WITH BLUE CHEESE TOPPING

3 envelopes unflavored gelatin
1 (46-ounce) can tomato juice, divided
2 tablespoons grated onion
½ teaspoon salt
1 cup chopped green pepper
1 cup chopped celery
Blue Cheese Topping

Soften gelatin in 1½ cups tomato juice; heat to dissolve gelatin. While warm, add onion, salt, and remaining tomato juice. Chill until slightly thickened; add green pepper and celery. Pour into a 9-cup mold and chill until firm. Serve with Blue Cheese Topping. Yield: 10 to 12 servings.

BLUE CHEESE TOPPING:

1 (3-ounce) package cream cheese, softened
3 tablespoons milk
1 (3-ounce) package blue cheese, crumbled

Combine cream cheese and milk; blend well. Add blue cheese and beat until thick. Yield: 1 cup.

TOMATO ASPIC WITH SHRIMP

2 envelopes unflavored gelatin
⅓ cup water
2½ cups tomato juice
¼ teaspoon salt
⅛ teaspoon pepper
Juice of 1 lemon
½ cup chopped celery
½ cup sliced pimiento-stuffed olives
1 pound shrimp, cooked, peeled, and deveined
Lettuce leaves
Cottage cheese
Sliced pimiento-stuffed olives (optional)

Dissolve gelatin in water; set aside. Combine tomato juice, salt, and pepper in a small saucepan; bring to a boil. Remove from heat; stir in gelatin; cool.

Stir in next 4 ingredients and pour into a lightly oiled 6-cup ring mold; chill until set.

Unmold on serving plate covered with lettuce leaves; fill center with cottage cheese. Garnish with sliced olives, if desired. Yield: 6 to 8 servings.

TOMATO-CUCUMBER-ONION SALAD

2 tablespoons vegetable oil
1 tablespoon vinegar
1 tablespoon sugar
½ teaspoon salt
¼ teaspoon pepper
1 teaspoon minced parsley
1 medium cucumber, peeled and thinly sliced
2 medium tomatoes, sliced
1 large onion, sliced and separated into rings

Combine first 6 ingredients in a jar; shake well. Combine vegetables in a serving bowl. Pour marinade over vegetables; refrigerate 2 hours before serving. Yield: 4 servings.
Mary Ann Turk,
Joplin, Mo.

TOSSED SALAD WITH FRENCH DRESSING

4 to 6 cups salad greens, torn into bite-size pieces
1 cup fresh spinach, torn into bite-size pieces
1 cup chopped celery
½ cup peeled and diced carrot
½ cup onion slices
½ cup coarsely chopped green pepper
1 cup cauliflower flowerets
Commercial French dressing

Combine vegetables; cover and chill until just before serving. Toss with French dressing and serve immediately. Yield: 8 servings.

MARINATED VEGETABLES

4 medium carrots, peeled and thinly sliced
1 cauliflower, broken into flowerets
1 large cucumber, peeled and thinly sliced
1 large onion, thinly sliced and separated into rings
4 radishes, sliced
2 stalks celery, sliced
1 (16-ounce) can green beans, drained
1 (15½-ounce) can kidney beans, drained
Italian Dressing

Cook carrots and cauliflower in boiling water about 5 minutes or until crisp-tender; drain well.

Place all ingredients except Italian Dressing in a large shallow dish; toss lightly. Pour Italian Dressing over vegetables; cover and chill overnight. Yield: 8 to 10 servings.

ITALIAN DRESSING:

¼ cup plus 2 tablespoons sugar
½ cup plus 2 tablespoons vinegar
½ cup plus 2 tablespoons water
½ cup catsup
½ cup vegetable oil
1½ teaspoons onion powder
1½ teaspoons salt
½ teaspoon dry mustard
½ teaspoon dried whole oregano
½ teaspoon paprika
⅛ teaspoon pepper
⅛ teaspoon garlic juice

Combine all ingredients in container of electric blender; blend well. Chill. Yield: about 2½ cups.
Mrs. Max E. Ayer,
Elizabethton, Tenn.

Tip: Use a stiff vegetable brush to scrub vegetables rather than peel them. Peeling is not necessary for many vegetables and causes a loss of vitamins found in and just under the skin.

MARINATED VEGETABLE SALAD

1 pound carrots, peeled, sliced, and cooked
1 green pepper, cut into rings
2 onions, cut into rings
1 cucumber, sliced
2 stalks celery, sliced
1 cup cauliflower flowerets
1 (10¾-ounce) can tomato soup, undiluted
1 cup sugar
¾ cup vinegar
¼ cup vegetable oil
1 tablespoon Worcestershire sauce
1 teaspoon pepper
1 teaspoon prepared mustard
¼ teaspoon salt

Combine vegetables in a large bowl. Stir together remaining ingredients; pour over vegetables. Cover and chill overnight. Yield: 10 to 12 servings.   *Lucille Blankenship,*
Hawkinsville, Ga.

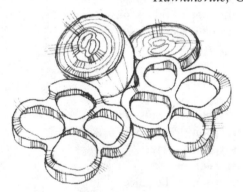

CHICKEN SALAD

3 cups cubed cooked chicken
1½ cups diced celery
3 hard-cooked eggs, chopped
3 sweet pickles, chopped
1 teaspoon salt
Mayonnaise

Combine chicken, celery, eggs, pickle, and salt; add enough mayonnaise to moisten. Yield: 6 to 8 servings.   *Debra Lancaster,*
Hawkinsville, Ga.

NEW ORLEANS SHRIMP SALAD

1 cup cooked rice
¾ pound fresh shrimp, cooked, peeled, and deveined
½ cup diced raw cauliflower
¼ cup minced onion
¼ cup chopped green pepper
¼ cup chopped celery
4 stuffed olives, sliced
½ cup mayonnaise
¼ cup French dressing
½ teaspoon salt
1 tablespoon lemon juice
Lettuce leaves

Combine all ingredients except lettuce; toss lightly. Chill thoroughly, and serve on lettuce leaves. Yield: 4 servings.

TROPICAL TUNA SALAD

2 avocados, peeled, halved, and seeded
1 tablespoon lemon juice
1 (6½-ounce) can chunk-style tuna, drained and flaked
½ cup diced celery
1 orange, peeled and sectioned
⅓ cup mayonnaise or salad dressing
Lettuce leaves
Sliced stuffed olives (optional)

Sprinkle avocados with lemon juice. Combine tuna, celery, orange sections, and mayonnaise; mix well. Spoon into avocado halves, and serve on lettuce leaves. Garnish with olives, if desired. Yield: 4 servings.

Round out your next family cookout or gathering with refreshing Crisp Coleslaw (page 54) and Marinated Vegetables (page 57).

Overleaf: A tall glass of sparkling Orange Blossom Punch (page 68) is one of the nicest ways to welcome a guest on a warm day.

Sandwiches, Snacks, and Beverages

CHEDDAR CHEESE BALL

2 (8-ounce) packages cream cheese, softened
2 cups (8 ounces) shredded Cheddar cheese
1 tablespoon chopped pimiento
1 tablespoon chopped green pepper
1 tablespoon minced onion
2 teaspoons Worcestershire sauce
1 teaspoon lemon juice
Dash of salt
Dash of red pepper
Chopped pecans

Combine all ingredients except pecans; mix well. Chill at least 1 hour. Shape into a ball, and coat with pecans. Yield: 1 cheese ball.

Sidnette Trimm,
Lyon, Miss.

CHILI DIP

1 pound ground beef
½ medium onion, chopped
1 (16-ounce) can refried beans
2 cups hot catsup
1 tablespoon chili powder
1 teaspoon salt
1 green onion, chopped
½ cup chopped black olives
½ cup (2 ounces) shredded Cheddar cheese

Brown beef and onion in a skillet over medium heat; drain. Add beans, catsup, chili powder, and salt to skillet; mix well. Bring to a boil; reduce heat, and simmer 20 to 30 minutes. Spoon into a fondue pot. Top with green onion, olives, and cheese. Keep warm. Serve with corn chips. Yield: about 3 cups.

GARDEN CHEESE DIP

1 (16-ounce) carton small-curd cottage cheese
1 (3-ounce) package cream cheese, softened
¼ cup finely chopped radishes
¼ cup finely chopped green onion
2 tablespoons chopped fresh parsley
1 clove garlic, crushed
¼ teaspoon salt
Dash of pepper

Combine all ingredients, mixing well. Chill. Serve with fresh vegetables. Yield: about 2½ cups.

Mrs. J. W. Hopkins,
Abilene, Tex.

BACON-HORSERADISH DIP

1 (8-ounce) carton commercial sour cream
3 tablespoons mayonnaise
2 to 3 teaspoons horseradish
¼ cup cooked, crumbled bacon
Dash of Worcestershire sauce
Salt to taste

Combine all ingredients, mixing well. Chill overnight. Serve with crisp, raw vegetables. Yield: 1¼ cups.

GREAT GUACAMOLE

4 avocados, peeled, seeded, and chopped
2 tomatoes, peeled and chopped
¼ cup chopped onion
1 teaspoon lemon juice
1 tablespoon mayonnaise
¼ teaspoon hot sauce
1½ teaspoons salt

Combine all ingredients in container of electric blender. Blend until smooth. Chill. Serve with chips. Yield: about 3 cups.

Note: Reserve 1 or 2 seeds from avocados. Place in dip to prevent mixture from darkening.

CHEESE ROUNDS

25 slices white bread
Melted butter or margarine
2 cups (8 ounces) shredded Cheddar cheese
1 small onion, minced
2 tablespoons butter or margarine, softened
2 teaspoons prepared mustard

Cut each slice of bread into 2 rounds using a 2-inch biscuit cutter. Toast rounds on one side. Brush untoasted sides with melted butter.
Combine cheese, onion, 2 tablespoons butter, and mustard, mixing well. Spread evenly onto buttered sides of rounds. Broil until cheese melts. Yield: 50 appetizers.

Mrs. Galen Johnson
Transylvania, La.

CRABMEAT BITES

1 (7-ounce) can crabmeat
½ cup butter or margarine, softened
1 (5-ounce) jar sharp process cheese spread
¼ teaspoon garlic salt
¼ teaspoon seasoned salt
1½ teaspoons mayonnaise
1 (12-ounce) package English muffins

Combine first 6 ingredients, blending well. Chill. Split muffins in half; spread with cheese mixture. Cut each muffin half into quarters. Yield: 4 dozen.

SHRIMP-STUFFED CELERY

1 (4½-ounce) can shrimp, drained and chopped
⅓ cup mayonnaise
¼ cup crushed pineapple
2 teaspoons minced parsley
1½ teaspoons lemon juice
1½ teaspoons finely chopped onion
1 tablespoon chopped walnuts
¼ teaspoon salt
Dash of hot sauce
2- to 3-inch celery sticks

Combine first 9 ingredients, mixing well; stuff mixture into celery sticks. Yield: 8 servings.

COCKTAIL MEATBALLS

2 pounds ground beef
½ cup dry breadcrumbs
¼ cup chopped onion
¼ cup milk
½ teaspoon salt
Dash of pepper
2 tablespoons vegetable oil
1 (12-ounce) bottle chili sauce
1 (10-ounce) jar grape jelly
Chopped green onion (optional)

Combine first 6 ingredients, mixing well; shape into 1-inch balls. Cook meatballs in hot oil in a large skillet until lightly browned; drain.
Combine chili sauce and jelly in skillet; cook over medium heat until jelly is melted. Add meatballs; simmer 15 to 20 minutes, stirring occasionally. Sprinkle with chopped green onion, if desired. Serve warm. Yield: about 5 dozen.

Mrs. Ellis Cowart,
Basile, La.

BLACK-EYED PEA COCKTAIL BALLS

1 (15-ounce) can black-eyed peas, drained and mashed
2 tablespoons grated onion
1 egg, beaten
1 tablespoon vegetable oil
About 5 tablespoons all-purpose flour
Ground red pepper to taste
¼ teaspoon salt
¼ teaspoon pepper
¼ teaspoon sage
Vegetable oil

Combine first 9 ingredients, mixing well. Drop by rounded teaspoonfuls into hot oil; cook until browned. Drain on paper towels. Yield: about 2 dozen.

PARTY PIZZAS

1 pound hot bulk sausage
1 (16-ounce) package process cheese spread, diced
¼ cup catsup
2 tablespoons Worcestershire sauce
1 teaspoon dried oregano leaves
1 teaspoon fennel seeds
2 (8-ounce) loaves sliced party rye bread

Brown sausage in a large skillet, stirring to crumble; drain. Add remaining ingredients, except bread; cook until cheese is melted, stirring constantly. Spread meat mixture evenly on bread slices; place on ungreased baking sheets. Bake at 350° for 10 minutes or until bubbly. Yield: about 6 dozen.   *Rachel V. Youree, Murfreesboro, Tenn.*

ORANGE ALMONDS

1½ cups whole blanched almonds, toasted
1 egg white, slightly beaten
¾ cup powdered sugar
1½ teaspoons grated orange rind
Dash of ground nutmeg

Combine almonds and egg white; set aside. Combine remaining ingredients. Drain almonds, and stir into sugar mixture until well coated. Spread on a greased baking sheet. Bake at 250° for 20 to 30 minutes or until coating is dry and nuts are crisp; stir occasionally. Yield: 1½ cups.

BARBECUED PECANS

2 tablespoons butter or margarine, melted
¼ cup Worcestershire sauce
1 tablespoon catsup
⅛ teaspoon hot sauce
4 cups pecan halves
Salt (optional)

Combine first 4 ingredients; stir in pecans, and mix well. Spread pecans evenly in a shallow baking pan. Bake at 300° for 30 minutes, stirring frequently. Drain on paper towels. Sprinkle with salt, if desired. Yield: 4 cups.

HOT DOG JUBILEE

6 frankfurters, finely chopped
½ cup (2 ounces) shredded Cheddar cheese
2 hard-cooked eggs, chopped
2 tablespoons chopped sweet pickle
3 tablespoons catsup
1 teaspoon prepared mustard
2 tablespoons vegetable oil
¼ teaspoon salt
6 hot dog buns, split

Combine frankfurters, cheese, eggs, and pickle. Combine catsup, mustard, oil, and salt; mix well and pour over frankfurter mixture. Toss lightly to mix. Spoon mixture into hot dog buns; wrap each in aluminum foil and bake at 350° for 25 minutes or until thoroughly heated. Yield: 6 sandwiches.   *Mrs. Bruce Fowler, Woodruff, S.C.*

Tip: Freeze very soft cheese 15 minutes to make shredding easier.

COZY CORN DOGS

½ cup all-purpose flour
½ cup cornmeal
1 teaspoon baking powder
½ teaspoon sugar
¾ teaspoon salt
½ teaspoon chili powder
1 egg, beaten
1½ teaspoons prepared mustard
⅓ to ½ cup milk
1 (16-ounce) package frankfurters
Vegetable oil

Combine flour, cornmeal, baking powder, sugar, salt, and chili powder; mix well and set aside.

Combine egg, mustard, and milk; mix well. Add cornmeal mixture and stir until smooth.

Insert a wooden skewer into one end of each frankfurter. Coat each frankfurter evenly with batter, allowing excess to drain; immediately fry in deep hot oil (375°) until golden brown. Serve hot. Yield: 8 to 10 servings.

Danelle Garrison,
Selma, Ala.

CRISPY CHICKEN SANDWICHES

1½ cups cooked chopped chicken
1 (10¾-ounce) can cream of mushroom soup, undiluted
1 (10¾-ounce) can cream of chicken soup, undiluted
2 tablespoons chopped pimiento
2 tablespoons chopped onion
1 (8-ounce) can sliced water chestnuts, drained
20 slices of bread, crusts removed
4 eggs, slightly beaten
2 tablespoons milk
1 (6-ounce) bag potato chips, crushed

Combine first 6 ingredients, mixing well. Spread evenly on 10 slices of bread; top with remaining 10 slices. Wrap individually in freezer wrap and freeze.

When ready to use sandwiches, combine eggs and milk; mix well. Dip each frozen sandwich into egg mixture and coat on all sides with crushed potato chips. Place on a lightly greased baking sheet and bake at 300° for 1 hour. Yield: 10 sandwiches.

Note: Sandwiches may be assembled, then wrapped individually in plastic freezer wrap and frozen until needed.
Jane Crum,
Morrilton, Ark.

DEVILED DELIGHT

1 (4-ounce) can deviled ham
2 hard-cooked eggs, finely chopped
3 tablespoons finely chopped dill pickle
1 teaspoon minced onion
1 teaspoon prepared mustard

Combine all ingredients; stir well. Chill. Spread on your favorite bread. Yield: about 1 cup.
Janice Finn,
Greensburg, Ky.

HOT CORNED BEEF SANDWICHES

1 (12-ounce) can corned beef
1 cup finely chopped celery
3 tablespoons hot dog relish
2 tablespoons chopped pimiento
⅓ cup mayonnaise
Seasoned pepper
10 hot dog or hamburger buns

Chop corned beef; stir in celery, relish, pimiento, and mayonnaise. Add seasoned pepper to taste. Fill buns with mixture and put on baking sheet (place hot dog buns with filled side up). Cover with foil; heat at 300° about 35 minutes. Yield: 10 sandwiches.

Tip: For a delicious way to use leftover hot dog buns, cut horizontally into thin slices, butter, sprinkle with Parmesan cheese or garlic powder, and toast until golden brown.

BARBECUED CORNED BEEF SANDWICHES

½ cup catsup
½ cup water
1 tablespoon cider vinegar
1 tablespoon Worcestershire sauce
1 teaspoon chili powder
⅛ teaspoon pepper
1 (12-ounce) can corned beef, coarsely
    chopped
4 hamburger buns, split and toasted

Combine first 6 ingredients in a skillet. Bring mixture just to boiling point. Add corned beef; reduce heat to low. Simmer 15 to 20 minutes, stirring frequently, until most of liquid is absorbed. Spoon corned beef mixture onto bottom half of buns; cover with bun tops. Yield: 4 servings.
Beth Dillard,
Cantonment, Fla.

DOUBLE BEEF SANDWICHES

12 slices rye bread
Softened butter or margarine
Prepared mustard
2 (2½-ounce) packages sliced dried beef
2 (3-ounce) packages sliced corned beef, or 1
    (12-ounce) can, cut into 12 slices
1 (6-ounce) package sliced Muenster or brick
    cheese
1 onion, thinly sliced
Dill pickle slices
Lettuce
Prepared horseradish
6 ripe olives

Spread bread with butter on one side; spread 6 slices of buttered bread with mustard and top with dried beef, corned beef, cheese, onion, pickle slices, and lettuce. Spread remaining 6 slices of buttered bread with horseradish and place on top of sandwiches. Secure each sandwich with a wooden pick and top with an olive. Yield: 6 servings. *Mrs. S. R. Griffith,*
Memphis, Tenn.

BEEFY CREAM CHEESE SANDWICH SPREAD

1 (2½-ounce) jar dried beef
2 (8-ounce) packages cream cheese, softened
2 tablespoons milk
1 tablespoon chopped green onion
½ teaspoon dillweed
¼ teaspoon hot sauce
¼ teaspoon salt
Pumpernickel bread

Cut beef into ½-inch strips; combine with next 6 ingredients, mixing until smooth. Chill and spread on pumpernickel bread. Yield: 2¼ cups.
Peggy Revels,
Woodruff, S.C.

BARBECUED BEEF SANDWICHES

1½ pounds ground beef
¾ cup finely chopped celery
¾ cup finely chopped onion
½ cup finely chopped green pepper
1 (8-ounce) can tomato sauce
¼ cup catsup
2 tablespoons brown sugar
2 tablespoons barbecue sauce
2 tablespoons vinegar
1 tablespoon prepared mustard
1 tablespoon Worcestershire sauce
1½ teaspoons salt
¼ teaspoon pepper
8 to 10 hamburger buns

Brown meat in large skillet; drain. Add celery, onion, and green pepper. Cook 5 minutes or until onion is tender. Add remaining ingredients except hamburger buns; cover, and simmer 1 hour. Serve on hamburger buns. Yield: 8 to 10 servings. *Sherry Smith,*
Afton, Tenn.

Tip: Prevent soggy sandwiches by spreading butter or margarine all the way to the crusts of the bread before adding filling.

OVEN BURGERS

1 cup catsup
½ cup water
¼ cup plus 2 tablespoons chopped onion
2 tablespoons sugar
3 tablespoons vinegar
2 tablespoons Worcestershire sauce
1½ pounds ground beef
¾ cup regular oats, uncooked
1 cup evaporated milk
3 tablespoons chopped onion
1½ teaspoons salt
¼ teaspoon pepper
10 hamburger buns

Combine first 6 ingredients in a medium saucepan; simmer 15 minutes. Set aside. Combine next 6 ingredients; mix well. Shape into 10 patties about ¾-inch thick. Cook patties over medium heat in a large skillet until browned, turning once.

Arrange patties in a 13- x 9- x 2-inch baking dish. Pour catsup mixture over patties. Bake at 350° about 40 minutes. Serve on buns. Yield: 10 servings. *Mrs. Al Van Loo, Norborne, Mo.*

EASY SLOPPY JOES

1 pound ground beef
1 medium onion, chopped
1 teaspoon salt
¼ teaspoon pepper
1 (10¾-ounce) can chicken gumbo soup, undiluted
1½ tablespoons catsup
1 tablespoon prepared mustard
6 to 8 hamburger buns

Combine ground beef, onion, salt, and pepper in a large skillet; cook until meat is lightly browned. Drain. Stir in soup, catsup, and mustard; simmer 15 minutes. Serve on buns. Yield: 6 to 8 servings. *Gayle Hurdle, Carthage, Miss.*

SUPER SLOPPY JOES

1 pound ground beef
2 teaspoons instant minced onion
1 (5¾-ounce) can mushroom steak sauce
1 (4-ounce) can tomato sauce
1 (2½-ounce) jar sliced mushrooms, drained
3 tablespoons chili sauce
1½ teaspoons chili powder
½ teaspoon salt
Dash of pepper
6 hamburger buns, buttered and toasted

Cook ground beef and onion until meat is browned; drain well. Add remaining ingredients, except buns; simmer 10 minutes, stirring occasionally. Spoon ground beef mixture onto bottom half of buns; cover with bun tops. Yield: 6 servings. *Ella Rae Poehls, Houston, Tex.*

HOT CHOCOLATE MIX

1 (25.6-ounce) package instant nonfat milk powder
1 (16-ounce) package instant chocolate-flavored mix
1 (6-ounce) jar non-dairy creamer
1 (16-ounce) package powdered sugar, sifted
¼ cup plus 2 tablespoons cocoa

Combine all ingredients in a large container. Store in a covered container. To serve, combine ⅓ cup mix with ⅔ cup boiling water and stir well. Yield: about 36 servings. *Elaine Gunter, Newport, Tenn.*

FLUFFY HOLIDAY EGGNOG

1 (32-ounce) can commercial eggnog
12 eggs, separated
1½ cups sugar
4 cups milk
4 cups whipping cream, whipped
Ground nutmeg

Pour commercial eggnog into a lightly oiled 4-cup ring mold; freeze. Remove from freezer 30 minutes before serving time to soften.

Beat egg yolks in a large mixing bowl until thick and lemon colored; gradually add sugar, beating well. Cover and chill at least 1 hour.

Stir milk into chilled mixture; fold in whipped cream. Beat egg whites (at room temperature) until stiff; fold into chilled mixture. Pour into punch bowl with eggnog ring. Sprinkle with nutmeg. Yield: about 5 quarts.

Mrs. Doug Hail,
Moody, Tex.

TOMATO TODDY

1 (10¾-ounce) can tomato soup, undiluted
1 (10½-ounce) can beef broth, undiluted
1¼ cups water
¼ teaspoon dried whole marjoram
¼ teaspoon dried whole thyme
Dash of hot sauce
Dash of Worcestershire sauce
1 tablespoon butter or margarine
Juice of 1 lime
Chopped parsley

Combine all ingredients except parsley in a saucepan; simmer 5 minutes. Garnish with parsley to serve. Yield: 8 (4-ounce) servings.

Rosemary Bowers,
Seminole, Tex.

STRAWBERRY SLUSH

3 (0.25-ounce) packages strawberry-flavored unsweetened soft drink mix
2 to 3 cups sugar
4 quarts water
3 cups pineapple juice
3 cups orange drink

Combine all ingredients, stirring to dissolve sugar; freeze. To serve, partially thaw. Yield: 5½ quarts. *Susan Smith,*
Bristol, Va.

ORANGE WASSAIL

1 cup sugar
1 cup water
1 dozen whole cloves
2 cinnamon sticks
3 quarts orange juice
1 (32-ounce) bottle cranberry juice

Combine sugar, water, and spices in a saucepan; simmer over low heat 10 minutes. Discard spices. Add juices to syrup. Heat and serve. Yield: 4 quarts.

MERRY BREW

½ cup firmly packed brown sugar
¼ teaspoon salt
2 sticks cinnamon
1 tablespoon whole cloves
½ teaspoon whole allspice
1 cup water
2 quarts apple juice
1 lemon, thinly sliced
1 orange, thinly sliced

Combine sugar, salt, spices, and water in a small saucepan; bring to a boil. Reduce heat; simmer 10 minutes. Combine apple juice and fruit slices in a large saucepan; heat gently. Strain hot spice liquid into apple juice, and serve warm. Yield: 2 quarts.

CRANAPPLE PUNCH

4 cups cranberry-apple juice
2 cups water
1 (6-ounce) can frozen lemonade concentrate, thawed and undiluted
3 tablespoons orange-flavored instant breakfast drink
3 cups ginger ale, chilled

Combine all ingredients except ginger ale; chill. Add ginger ale just before serving. Yield: about 2½ quarts. *Mrs. James Cook,*
Columbia, La.

ORANGE BLOSSOM PUNCH

6 cups orange juice
1 cup lemon juice
⅓ cup maraschino cherry juice
½ cup sugar
1 (33.8-ounce) bottle ginger ale, chilled
Fresh strawberries (optional)

Combine juice and sugar, mixing well. When ready to serve, add ginger ale; serve over ice. Garnish with fresh strawberries, if desired. Yield: about 3 quarts. *Mabel B. Couch, Chelsea, Okla.*

ORANGE SHERBET PARTY PUNCH

2 (3-ounce) packages strawberry-flavored gelatin
1½ cups sugar
2 cups boiling water
2 cups cold water
1 (46-ounce) can pineapple juice
1 (46-ounce) can orange juice
1 cup lemon juice
½ gallon orange sherbet, softened
1 (33.8-ounce) bottle ginger ale, chilled

Combine gelatin and sugar; add boiling water and stir until dissolved. Stir in cold water and juice; chill. Spoon sherbet into punch; add ginger ale. Yield: about 6½ quarts.

Barbara Anz, Clifton, Tex.

LIME-PINEAPPLE PUNCH

1 cup sugar
2 cups water, divided
2 teaspoons grated lime rind
½ cup lime juice
1 pint pineapple sherbet
1 pint lime sherbet
3½ cups lemon-lime carbonated beverage

Combine sugar and 1 cup water in a medium saucepan; cook, stirring constantly, until sugar dissolves. Add remaining 1 cup water, lime rind, and lime juice; chill. Spoon sherbet into punch; add lemon-lime beverage. Yield: about 2½ quarts. *Mickie Morrow, Bernice, La.*

TANGY PUNCH

2½ cups orange-flavored instant breakfast drink
3 quarts water
2 (46-ounce) cans pineapple juice, chilled
1 (6-ounce) can frozen lemonade concentrate, thawed and undiluted
4 (33.8-ounce) bottles ginger ale, chilled

Dissolve breakfast drink in water; add pineapple juice and lemonade concentrate. Chill. To serve, pour mixture over ice; stir in ginger ale. Yield: about 2½ gallons.

Mrs. Nelson Jones, Richlands, N.C.

HOT SPICED FRUIT PUNCH

2 teaspoons whole cloves
2 (4-inch) sticks cinnamon, broken
1 (46-ounce) can pineapple-grapefruit juice
3 cups orange juice
1 cup water
½ cup firmly packed brown sugar
Pinch of salt

Place cloves and cinnamon in center of a small piece of cheesecloth; tie securely. Place spice bag and remaining ingredients in a large saucepan; stir to blend well. Cook over medium heat 30 to 40 minutes. Remove spice bag. Serve hot. Yield: 10 cups. *Jean Moore, Staunton, Va.*

What a beautiful table for a holiday party! Clockwise from front: Cheddar Cheese Ball (page 61), Cherry Winks (page 21), Garden Cheese Dip (page 61), Cocktail Meatballs (page 62), and cups of Fluffy Holiday Eggnog (page 66).

Overleaf: Corn and Okra Combo (page 76) is just one of many ways to enjoy fresh sweet corn.

Side Dishes and Vegetables

BEST BAKED BEANS

1 (28-ounce) can pork and beans
¼ cup catsup
3 tablespoons brown sugar
1 small onion, diced
2 tablespoons cooked and crumbled bacon
½ teaspoon chili powder
½ teaspoon dry mustard
Dash of red pepper
¼ teaspoon garlic salt
1 medium onion, sliced

Combine all ingredients except sliced onion in a greased 1½-quart casserole. Stir well and top with onion slices. Bake at 350° for 1 hour. Yield: 4 to 6 servings.

SPANISH-STYLE GREEN BEANS

1 pound fresh green beans
½ cup chopped green pepper
¼ cup chopped onion
1 tablespoon vegetable or olive oil
2 medium tomatoes, peeled and chopped
¼ to ½ teaspoon dried whole basil
¼ teaspoon dried whole rosemary
½ to 1 teaspoon salt
¼ teaspoon pepper

Remove strings from beans; wash beans thoroughly. Cut beans into 1½-inch pieces.

Cook beans in boiling salted water 15 to 20 minutes or until crisp-tender. Drain and set aside.

Sauté green pepper and onion in hot oil until tender. Add tomatoes, basil, rosemary, salt, pepper, and beans, mixing well. Heat thoroughly. Yield: 6 to 8 servings.

Treva Musick,
Tolar, Tex.

GREEN BEANS WITH ZUCCHINI

1 pound fresh green beans
¼ cup butter or margarine
½ cup minced onion
2 medium zucchini, cut into ¼-inch slices
4 slices bacon, cooked and crumbled
¾ teaspoon salt
Dash of pepper

Remove strings from beans; wash beans thoroughly. Cut beans into 1½-inch pieces. Wash thoroughly. Cook beans in boiling salted water 15 to 20 minutes or until crisp-tender. Drain.

Melt butter in a large skillet; add onion and sauté about 3 minutes. Add zucchini and cook over medium-high heat 3 to 4 minutes, stirring constantly. Stir in beans, bacon, salt, and pepper; cook 1 minute. Yield: 6 servings.

Dorothy Youk,
Durham, Kans.

CANNING GREEN BEANS

Wash beans, trim ends, and string if necessary; cut into 1-inch lengths.

Hot pack: Cover beans with boiling water, and boil 5 minutes. Pack beans loosely in hot sterilized jars, leaving ½-inch headspace. Add ½ teaspoon salt to pints, 1 teaspoon to quarts. Cover with boiling liquid, leaving ½-inch headspace. Cover at once with metal lids, and screw bands tight. Process in pressure canner at 10 pounds pressure (240°). Process pint jars for 20 minutes and quart jars for 25 minutes.

Cold pack: Pack beans tightly into hot sterilized jars, leaving ½-inch headspace. Add ½ teaspoon salt to pints, 1 teaspoon to quarts. Cover with boiling water, leaving ½-inch headspace. Cover at once with metal lids, and screw bands tight. Process in pressure canner at 10 pounds of pressure (240°). Process pints for 20 minutes and quarts for 25 minutes.

HARVARD BEETS

12 medium beets
¼ cup sugar
1 tablespoon cornstarch
¼ teaspoon salt
½ cup vinegar
¼ cup grape jelly
2 tablespoons butter or margarine
1 teaspoon grated orange rind

Leave root and 1 inch of stem on beets; scrub with a brush. Place beets in a saucepan; add water to cover. Bring to a boil; cover and cook 35 to 40 minutes or until tender. Drain. Trim off beet stems and roots, and rub off skins; cut beets into ¼-inch slices.

Combine sugar, cornstarch, and salt in a saucepan. Blend in vinegar and jelly. Cook over medium heat, stirring constantly, until thickened and smooth. Add beets and butter; heat well, stirring occasionally. Garnish with orange rind. Yield: 6 servings.

Tip: A clean toothbrush is a handy gadget to aid in removal of all bits of grated rind from grater.

BEETS WITH PINEAPPLE

2 tablespoons brown sugar
1 tablespoon cornstarch
¼ teaspoon salt
1 (8¼-ounce) can pineapple chunks
1 tablespoon butter or margarine
1 tablespoon lemon juice
8 to 10 small beets, cooked, peeled, and sliced, or 1 (16-ounce) can sliced beets, drained

Combine brown sugar, cornstarch, and salt in a medium saucepan. Drain pineapple, reserving juice. Stir pineapple juice into brown sugar mixture. Cook over medium heat, stirring constantly, until mixture thickens and bubbles. Stir in butter and lemon juice. Add beets and pineapple. Cook about 5 minutes or until thoroughly heated. Yield: 4 servings.

BROCCOLI GOLDENROD

¾ pound fresh broccoli
½ cup mayonnaise
1 tablespoon lemon juice
½ teaspoon grated onion
⅛ teaspoon ground thyme
3 hard-cooked egg yolks, sieved

Cook broccoli in a small amount of boiling salted water just until tender. Drain and set aside.

Combine next 4 ingredients in a saucepan, and heat thoroughly. Pour over broccoli; sprinkle with egg yolk. Yield: 4 to 6 servings.

BROCCOLI WITH CHOWDER SAUCE

2 pounds fresh broccoli or 3 (10-ounce) packages frozen broccoli
1 (10¾-ounce) can New England clam chowder, undiluted
½ cup commercial sour cream
½ teaspoon salt
¾ cup (3 ounces) shredded Cheddar cheese

Cook broccoli in a small amount of boiling salted water just until tender; drain well. Arrange broccoli in a buttered 13- x 9- x 2-inch baking dish, and set aside.

Combine chowder, sour cream, and salt, mixing well; spoon over broccoli. Bake at 325° for 20 minutes. Remove from oven and sprinkle with cheese; bake 2 minutes longer or until cheese melts. Yield: 8 to 10 servings.

BROCCOLI-RICE CASSEROLE

2 (10-ounce) packages frozen chopped broccoli
1 small onion, chopped
2 tablespoons butter or margarine
1 (10¾-ounce) can cream of chicken soup, undiluted
½ cup milk
1 (8-ounce) package process American cheese spread, cubed
3 cups cooked rice

Cook broccoli according to package directions; drain well and set aside.

Sauté onion in butter until tender. Add soup, milk, and cheese; cook over medium heat, stirring constantly, until cheese melts. Stir in rice and broccoli; pour into a greased 2-quart shallow casserole. Bake at 350° for 30 minutes. Yield: 6 to 8 servings. *Trudys L. Pittman, Corinth, Miss.*

CABBAGE AU GRATIN

4 cups shredded cabbage
2 tablespoons butter or margarine, melted
1½ tablespoons all-purpose flour
½ teaspoon salt
1 cup milk
1 cup (4 ounces) shredded Cheddar cheese
2 cups soft breadcrumbs
¼ cup butter or margarine, melted

Boil cabbage in water to cover for 5 minutes; drain well.

Combine 2 tablespoons melted butter, flour, and salt in a saucepan; cook over low heat, stirring constantly, until bubbly. Gradually add milk; cook, stirring constantly, until smooth and thickened.

Alternate layers of cabbage, cheese, and white sauce in a greased 1½-quart casserole. Combine breadcrumbs and ¼ cup melted butter; sprinkle crumbs over casserole. Bake at 350° for 25 minutes. Yield: 6 servings.

CABBAGE CHOP SUEY

2 tablespoons shortening
3 cups shredded cabbage
1 cup thinly sliced celery
1 cup thinly sliced green pepper
1 medium onion, thinly sliced
1½ teaspoons salt
¼ teaspoon pepper
Chow mein noodles (optional)

Heat shortening in a large skillet over medium heat. Add vegetables, tossing lightly. Cover and cook over low heat 5 minutes. Add salt and pepper; cook, uncovered, 1 minute, stirring gently. Sprinkle with chow mein noodles, if desired. Serve immediately. Yield: 5 to 6 servings. *Marilyn Hershberger, Due West, S.C.*

OVEN CABBAGE

1 medium head cabbage
1 tablespoon plus 1 teaspoon bacon drippings, divided
Salt and pepper
½ cup water, divided
3 tablespoons picante sauce, divided

Remove and discard large outer leaves of cabbage. Cut head into 4 wedges. Place each wedge on a piece of aluminum foil. Spread each wedge with 1 teaspoon bacon drippings; sprinkle with salt and pepper.

Wrap foil tightly around cabbage, leaving one end open. Spoon 2 tablespoons water and 2¼ teaspoons picante sauce into each packet. Seal tightly. Bake at 350° for 1 hour or until cabbage is tender. Yield: 4 servings.

ORANGE-GLAZED CARROTS

2 pounds carrots
1½ cups water
1 teaspoon salt
1 teaspoon grated orange rind
¼ cup butter or margarine
¼ cup firmly packed brown sugar
½ teaspoon ground cardamom

Peel carrots; cut in quarters lengthwise and in half crosswise. Bring water and salt to a boil; add carrots. Cover and cook 10 to 15 minutes or until tender; drain.

Add remaining ingredients to carrots. Gently stir over low heat until butter is melted and carrots are glazed. Yield: 8 servings.

PICKLED CARROTS

2 pounds carrots, peeled and cut into
    3- x ¼-inch strips
1½ cups sugar
1½ cups vinegar
1½ cups water
¼ cup whole mustard seeds
3 (½-inch) cinnamon sticks
3 whole cloves

Cover and cook carrots about 15 minutes in a small amount of boiling, salted water. Drain; place carrots in a glass or plastic container.

Combine remaining ingredients in a saucepan; bring to a boil, and simmer 20 minutes. Pour over carrots, and toss well. Cover tightly; refrigerate overnight. Yield: 10 to 12 servings.
Bobby McVey,
Plainview, Tex.

CHEESY CAULIFLOWER

3 tablespoons butter or margarine
3 tablespoons all-purpose flour
1 cup milk
1 teaspoon salt
¼ teaspoon pepper
1½ cups (6 ounces) shredded sharp Cheddar
    cheese, divided
5 (10-ounce) packages frozen cauliflower,
    cooked and drained

Melt butter in a heavy saucepan over low heat; add flour, stirring until smooth. Cook 1 minute, stirring constantly. Gradually add milk; cook over medium heat, stirring constantly, until thickened and bubbly. Stir in salt and pepper. Remove from heat; stir in 1 cup cheese, and set aside.

Place cauliflower in a greased 2½-quart casserole. Pour cheese sauce over cauliflower. Sprinkle remaining ½ cup cheese over top. Bake at 350° for 30 minutes. Yield: about 12 servings.
Mrs. Jack M. Moore,
Staunton, Va.

SCALLOPED CAULIFLOWER

1 medium head cauliflower
1 cup coarsely chopped corned beef
3 tablespoons butter or margarine, melted
3 tablespoons all-purpose flour
1½ cups milk
½ teaspoon salt
¼ teaspoon pepper
2 cups (8 ounces) shredded Cheddar cheese,
    divided
2 tablespoons buttered breadcrumbs

Wash cauliflower and remove green leaves; break into flowerets. Cook, covered, in a small amount of boiling water 10 minutes; drain. Place cauliflower in a 2-quart casserole; sprinkle with corned beef.

Combine butter and flour in a small saucepan, mixing well; cook over low heat until bubbly. Slowly add milk; cook, stirring constantly, until smooth and thickened. Add salt and pepper. Add 1½ cups cheese, stirring until cheese melts. Pour over corned beef.

Bake at 350° for 10 minutes; sprinkle with remaining ½ cup cheese and breadcrumbs. Bake an additional 10 minutes. Yield: 4 servings.

CHEESE-TOPPED CAULIFLOWER

1 head cauliflower
¾ cup (3 ounces) shredded sharp Cheddar cheese
½ cup mayonnaise
2 teaspoons Dijon mustard

Remove large outer leaves of cauliflower. Break cauliflower into flowerets and wash thoroughly. Cook in boiling salted water 8 to 10 minutes or until crisp-tender; drain.

Combine cheese, mayonnaise, and mustard; mix well.

Arrange cauliflower in a buttered 1½-quart baking dish. Spoon cheese mixture evenly over top. Bake at 350° for 10 minutes or until cheese is melted. Yield: 4 to 6 servings.

Fay Crow,
Clinton, Ark.

FRENCH-FRIED CAULIFLOWER

1 large head cauliflower
1 cup dry breadcrumbs
1 tablespoon grated Parmesan cheese
1 clove garlic, minced
2 tablespoons chopped parsley
2 tablespoons chopped celery leaves
½ teaspoon salt
¼ teaspoon pepper
2 eggs, beaten
Vegetable oil

Wash cauliflower, and remove green leaves. Break into flowerets. Cook, covered, in a small amount of boiling salted water 8 to 10 minutes or just until tender; drain well.

Combine breadcrumbs, cheese, garlic, parsley, celery leaves, salt, and pepper; set aside. Dip cauliflower in egg; coat with breadcrumb mixture. Cook in oil heated to 375° about 10 minutes or until lightly browned. Yield: 4 servings.

FAR EAST CELERY

4 cups (1-inch) celery slices
1 (8-ounce) can water chestnuts, drained and sliced
1 (10¾-ounce) can cream of chicken soup, undiluted
¼ cup chopped pimiento
¼ teaspoon salt
½ cup chow mein noodles
¼ cup slivered almonds
2 tablespoons butter or margarine, melted

Cook celery in a small amount of boiling salted water about 6 to 8 minutes or just until tender; drain. Combine celery with water chestnuts, soup, pimiento, and salt; mix well, and pour the mixture into a lightly greased 2-quart casserole.

Combine chow mein noodles, almonds, and butter; toss lightly, and sprinkle over celery mixture. Bake at 350° for 35 minutes. Yield: 6 servings.

SCALLOPED CELERY

2 cups (1-inch) celery slices
1 (11-ounce) can Cheddar cheese soup, undiluted
Hot sauce to taste
½ cup soft breadcrumbs
½ cup (2 ounces) shredded Cheddar cheese

Cook celery in a small amount of boiling salted water about 10 minutes or just until tender; drain. Stir in soup and hot sauce; mix well.

Spoon mixture into a greased 1½-quart casserole; sprinkle with breadcrumbs and Cheddar cheese. Bake at 350° for 25 to 30 minutes. Yield: 4 to 6 servings.

Side Dishes and Vegetables 75

CORN AND GREEN BEAN CASSEROLE

2¼ cups frozen white shoepeg corn
1 (16-ounce) package frozen French-style
   green beans
½ cup chopped onion
½ cup chopped celery
½ cup chopped green pepper
3 tablespoons butter or margarine, melted
   and divided
½ cup (2 ounces) shredded sharp Cheddar
   cheese
1 (10¾-ounce) can cream of celery soup,
   undiluted
½ cup commercial sour cream
Dash of salt
⅛ teaspoon pepper
½ cup round, buttery cracker crumbs
1 tablespoon slivered almonds (optional)

Cook frozen vegetables according to package directions; drain well.

Sauté onion, celery, and green pepper in 2 tablespoons butter until tender. Combine sautéed mixture, corn, beans, cheese, soup, sour cream, salt, and pepper; stir well and spoon into a greased 2-quart casserole.

Combine cracker crumbs, remaining butter, and almonds, if desired. Stir well. Sprinkle crumb mixture over casserole. Bake at 350° for 45 minutes. Yield: 6 to 8 servings.

Frances Counts Boland,
Pomaria, S.C.

CORN AND OKRA COMBO

6 ears fresh corn
1 beef-flavored bouillon cube
½ cup boiling water
1 medium onion, sliced and separated into
   rings
2 medium-size green peppers, coarsely
   chopped
¼ cup butter or margarine
1 (10-ounce) package frozen cut okra, thawed
¾ teaspoon salt
⅛ teaspoon pepper

Remove husks and silks from corn. Cut corn from cob, scraping cob to remove pulp; set aside. Dissolve bouillon cube in boiling water; set aside. Sauté onion and green pepper in butter until crisp-tender. Add remaining ingredients; mix well. Bring to a boil; reduce heat, cover, and simmer 5 to 10 minutes or until tender, stirring often. Yield: 8 servings.

Linda McLauchlin,
Beaumont, Tex.

SAUTEED CORN WITH BACON

6 ears fresh corn
4 slices bacon
1 teaspoon salt
¼ teaspoon pepper

Remove husks and silks from corn. Cut corn from cob, scraping cob to remove pulp; set aside. Cook bacon in a large skillet until crisp; remove bacon, reserving drippings. Crumble bacon and set aside. Sauté corn in bacon drippings until golden brown. Add water to cover, salt, and pepper. Bring to a boil; reduce heat, cover, and simmer 30 to 45 minutes. Stir in crumbled bacon. Yield: 6 to 8 servings.

Susie F. Wilhite,
Monroe, La.

SOUTHERN-STYLE CREAMED CORN

8 ears fresh corn
2 tablespoons all-purpose flour
2 tablespoons sugar
1 teaspoon salt
½ cup milk
¼ cup plus 2 tablespoons butter or margarine
½ cup whipping cream

Remove husks and silks from corn. Cut corn from cob, scraping cob to remove pulp; set aside. Combine flour, sugar, and salt in a small bowl; gradually stir in milk until mixture is smooth. Melt butter in a heavy skillet; add corn, mixing well. Gradually stir in flour mixture; cover and cook over low heat 10 minutes, stirring often. Stir in whipping cream; serve immediately. Yield: 8 servings.

Mattie P. Beavers,
Cedar Bluff, Va.

SWISS CORN BAKE

6 ears fresh corn
½ cup water
1 egg, beaten
1 cup (4 ounces) shredded Swiss cheese, divided
1 (5.33-ounce) can evaporated milk
2 tablespoons finely chopped onion
½ teaspoon salt
Dash of pepper
1 teaspoon butter or margarine, melted
½ cup soft breadcrumbs

Remove husks and silks from corn. Cut corn from cob, scraping cob to remove pulp. Combine corn and water in a saucepan; bring to a boil, reduce heat, and simmer 5 minutes, stirring often. Drain. Add egg, ¾ cup cheese, milk, onion, salt, and pepper; mix well, and spoon into a greased 10- x 6- x 2-inch baking dish. Set aside.

Combine butter, breadcrumbs, and remaining cheese; mix well, and sprinkle over corn mixture. Bake at 350° for 25 minutes. Yield: 8 servings. *Mrs. Edward M. Vernon,*
Blanch, N.C.

CRANBERRY RELISH

4 cups fresh cranberries
2 oranges, unpeeled
2 cups sugar
1 (3-ounce) package lemon-flavored gelatin
1½ cups boiling water
½ cup chopped celery
½ cup chopped pecans

Carefully sort and wash cranberries; drain. Quarter and seed oranges. Coarsely grind cranberries and oranges in a food grinder or processor. Combine cranberry mixture and sugar; stir well and let stand until sugar dissolves.

Dissolve gelatin in boiling water; cool. Add gelatin, celery, and pecans to cranberry mixture; stir well. Chill. Yield: 2 quarts.

Mrs. Charles Cron,
Brandenburg, Ky.

FRIED EGGPLANT PARMESAN

1 large eggplant
1 cup all-purpose flour
1 cup milk
1 egg, beaten
1 teaspoon baking powder
1 teaspoon salt
Dash of pepper
Vegetable oil
Parmesan cheese

Peel eggplant; cut into ¼-inch slices.
Combine next 6 ingredients, mixing well. Dip eggplant into batter. Fry in hot oil (375°) in a large skillet until golden brown. Drain; sprinkle with Parmesan cheese. Yield: 6 servings.

Mrs. Melvin J. Cheatham,
Gladys, Va.

EGGPLANT ITALIAN

1 large eggplant
1 egg, beaten
⅔ cup fine breadcrumbs
Vegetable oil
Salt and pepper to taste
1 teaspoon ground oregano
2 tablespoons chopped parsley
¼ cup grated Parmesan cheese
1 (8-ounce) can tomato sauce
Sliced mozzarella cheese

Peel eggplant, and cut into ½-inch slices. Dip slices into egg, and coat with breadcrumbs. Sauté in hot oil until lightly browned.

Overlap slices in a greased 10- x 6- x 2-inch baking dish. Sprinkle with salt, pepper, oregano, parsley, and Parmesan cheese. Pour tomato sauce over eggplant slices; cover with mozzarella cheese slices. Bake at 350° for 20 minutes. Yield: about 6 servings.

SPANISH EGGPLANT

1 medium eggplant, peeled and cut into
½-inch slices
½ cup chopped onion
½ cup chopped green pepper
¼ cup bacon drippings
1 (16-ounce) can whole tomatoes, undrained
and quartered
1½ teaspoons salt
2 tablespoons sugar
½ cup dry breadcrumbs
½ cup grated Parmesan cheese

Combine eggplant, onion, green pepper, and bacon drippings; mix well, and let stand 10 minutes. Stir in tomatoes, salt, and sugar. Place in a medium saucepan; cover and cook 5 to 10 minutes over low heat.

Spoon mixture into a greased, shallow 2-quart casserole; sprinkle with breadcrumbs and cheese. Bake at 350° for 20 minutes. Yield: 6 to 8 servings.

GRITS AND CHEESE CASSEROLE

1½ cups uncooked regular grits
6 cups boiling water
1 teaspoon salt
½ cup butter or margarine
1 pound process American cheese spread,
diced
¼ teaspoon hot sauce
3 eggs, beaten

Stir grits into boiling water; add salt. Return to a boil. Reduce heat and simmer 4 minutes, stirring frequently, until thickened. Remove from heat. Add butter, cheese, and hot sauce, stirring until butter and cheese melt.

Gradually stir about one-fourth of hot grits mixture into eggs; add to remaining hot mixture, stirring constantly. Pour into a buttered 10- x 6- x 2-inch baking dish. Bake at 350° for 1 hour. Yield: about 6 servings.

Mrs. Ausy P. Brown,
San Antonio, Tex.

NASSAU GRITS

8 slices bacon
1 medium onion, chopped
2 small green peppers, finely chopped
1 (16-ounce) can tomatoes, undrained and
chopped
¼ teaspoon sugar
1½ cups uncooked regular grits
6 cups boiling water
1 teaspoon salt

Cook bacon in a skillet until crisp; drain, crumble, and set aside. Drain drippings, reserving 2 tablespoons in skillet.

Sauté onion and green pepper in drippings; stir in tomatoes and sugar. Bring to a boil; reduce heat and simmer 30 minutes, stirring occasionally.

Stir grits into boiling water; add salt. Cook 10 to 20 minutes, stirring frequently, until grits are thickened. Remove from heat; stir in tomato mixture. Spoon into serving dish; sprinkle bacon on top. Yield: 8 servings.

Sarah Hestle Countryman,
Monroeville, Ala.

OKRA-ONION CASSEROLE

2 cups sliced okra
1 small onion, chopped
1 cup buttered breadcrumbs, divided
½ cup (2 ounces) shredded Cheddar cheese
2 tablespoons butter or margarine, melted
1 egg, beaten
½ teaspoon salt
½ teaspoon pepper

Combine all ingredients except ¼ cup buttered breadcrumbs. Spoon into a lightly greased 1½-quart casserole. Bake at 350° for 30 minutes. Sprinkle with reserved buttered breadcrumbs, and bake 5 additional minutes. Yield: 4 servings.

Tip: Crumble extra pieces of cooked bacon and freeze. Use as a topping for casseroles or baked potatoes.

OVEN-FRIED OKRA

¼ cup cornmeal
1 teaspoon salt
¼ teaspoon pepper
6 cups (½-inch-thick) sliced okra
1 tablespoon vegetable oil or bacon drippings

Combine cornmeal, salt, and pepper; stir well.

Dredge okra in cornmeal mixture. Spread oil in a 15- x 10- x 1-inch pan; spread okra evenly in pan. Bake at 400° for 30 to 45 minutes, stirring often. Yield: 10 to 12 servings.

SAUCY PEPPER SKILLET

2 medium onions, sliced and separated into rings
2 tablespoons vegetable oil
3 large green peppers, sliced into rings
1 (4-ounce) can mushroom stems and pieces, drained
½ cup commercial Italian cooking sauce
1 teaspoon garlic powder
1 teaspoon seasoned salt
1 teaspoon dried whole oregano
1 teaspoon dried basil leaves

Sauté onion in hot oil in a large skillet for 1 minute, stirring occasionally. Add remaining ingredients, mixing well. Reduce heat; cover, and simmer 20 to 25 minutes, stirring occasionally. Yield: 6 to 8 servings.
Peggy Fowler Revels,
Woodruff, S.C.

CHEESY NEW POTATOES WITH BACON

12 medium-size new potatoes
8 slices bacon, cooked and crumbled
1 cup (4 ounces) shredded Cheddar cheese
½ cup butter or margarine, melted
1 teaspoon salt
¼ teaspoon pepper

Wash potatoes thoroughly; do not peel. Place potatoes in a small Dutch oven; cover with water. Bring to a boil; reduce heat and cook 20 minutes or until tender. Drain well and cool slightly. Cut into ¼-inch slices.

Layer half of all ingredients in order listed in a greased 2-quart casserole. Repeat layers. Bake at 400° for 15 minutes or until thoroughly heated. Yield: 6 to 8 servings.
Mrs. Gwen Granderson,
Kingsland, Ark.

SCALLOPED POTATO BAKE

3 tablespoons butter or margarine
3 tablespoons all-purpose flour
2 cups milk
4 to 5 large baking potatoes, peeled and cut into ¼-inch slices
1 large onion, chopped
1 cup cubed, cooked ham
1 teaspoon salt
¼ teaspoon pepper
4 cups (16 ounces) shredded process American cheese

Melt butter in a heavy saucepan over low heat; add flour, stirring until smooth. Cook 1 minute, stirring constantly. Gradually stir in milk; cook over medium heat, stirring constantly, until thickened and bubbly.

Layer half each of potato slices, onion, ham, salt, pepper, cheese, and white sauce in a greased 2½-quart casserole; repeat layers. Cover and bake at 350° for 1 hour and 15 minutes. Yield: 8 servings. *Mrs. Steve Toney,*
Helena, Ark.

Side Dishes and Vegetables 79

SAVORY STUFFED POTATOES

5 or 6 medium potatoes
Butter
⅓ cup butter or margarine
½ cup milk
½ cup commercial sour cream
2 teaspoons salt
⅛ teaspoon pepper
2 tablespoons grated Parmesan cheese
Chopped chives

Wash potatoes and rub skins with butter. Bake at 425° for 1 hour or until done.

Allow potatoes to cool to touch. Slice skin away from top of each potato. Carefully scoop out pulp, leaving shells intact; spoon pulp into a mixing bowl. Add ⅓ cup butter, milk, sour cream, salt, and pepper; mash potatoes until fluffy. Stuff shells with potato mixture. Sprinkle with cheese; bake at 425° for 15 minutes. Remove from oven, and top with chives. Yield: 5 to 6 servings.
Mrs. Doug Hail,
Moody, Tex.

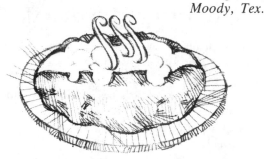

ORANGE-STUFFED SWEET POTATOES

4 medium-size sweet potatoes
¼ cup orange juice
2 medium oranges, peeled, sectioned, and seeded
¼ cup brown sugar, divided
Ground nutmeg

Scrub potatoes; cut an x-shape about 1½ inches long and 1 inch deep in each potato. Brush potatoes with orange juice. Fill slits with orange sections; top each with 1 tablespoon brown sugar and a dash of nutmeg. Wrap each

in aluminum foil; bake at 375° for 1 hour or until potatoes are done. Yield: 4 servings.
Ann Whitfield,
Corinth, Miss.

SWEET POTATO CRISP

6 medium-size sweet potatoes
½ cup margarine
¼ cup all-purpose flour
½ cup firmly packed brown sugar
1½ teaspoons freshly ground pepper
¼ cup evaporated milk
¼ cup finely chopped pecans

Cook sweet potatoes in boiling water 20 to 25 minutes or until tender; peel, and slice crosswise into ½-inch pieces. Place in a shallow, greased 1½-quart casserole.

Cut margarine into flour and brown sugar until mixture resembles coarse crumbs; add pepper, milk, and pecans. Mix well and spread over potatoes. Broil 6 inches from heat until bubbly, about 6 minutes. Yield: 6 servings.
Rebecca Ashley,
Afton, Tenn.

ORANGE-GLAZED SWEET POTATOES

8 medium-size sweet potatoes
1¼ teaspoons salt, divided
2 tablespoons butter or margarine
1 tablespoon grated orange rind
¾ cup dark corn syrup

Wash and scrub sweet potatoes. Add 1 teaspoon salt to boiling water; cook potatoes in water until tender, about 30 to 40 minutes. Peel and cut in half. Arrange potatoes in a shallow baking dish; set aside.

Combine remaining ¼ teaspoon salt, butter, orange rind, and corn syrup in a small saucepan. Bring to a boil; spoon over sweet potatoes. Bake at 350° for 30 minutes, basting potatoes occasionally with syrup. Yield: 8 to 10 servings.

YUMMY YAMS

4 pounds sweet potatoes, cooked and mashed
½ cup butter or margarine, melted
¼ cup bourbon
⅓ cup orange juice
⅓ cup firmly packed brown sugar
¾ teaspoon salt
½ teaspoon apple pie spice
½ to ¾ cup pecan halves

Combine all ingredients except pecans in a large mixing bowl, mixing well. Pour into a greased 2½-quart casserole; arrange pecans around edge of dish. Bake at 350° for 45 minutes. Yield: 8 to 10 servings.

RICE MEDLEY

2 cups uncooked instant rice
3 medium carrots, cut into 2-inch strips
1 cup chopped onion
1 bunch scallions or green onions, cut into
    1-inch lengths
½ cup seedless raisins
¼ cup plus 1 tablespoon butter or margarine,
    divided
2 cups water
1 (10-ounce) package frozen English peas
2 teaspoons salt
1 cup pecan halves

Combine first 5 ingredients; sauté in ¼ cup butter about 5 minutes or until rice is lightly browned, stirring frequently. Add water, peas, and salt; bring to a boil, separating frozen peas. Reduce heat; cover and simmer 5 minutes.

Sauté pecans lightly in remaining butter; stir into rice mixture. Yield: 8 servings.

ORANGE RICE

2 cups water
1 tablespoon grated orange rind
½ cup orange juice
1 teaspoon salt
1 cup uncooked regular rice

Combine first 4 ingredients in a medium saucepan. Bring to a boil; add rice. Cover; reduce heat and simmer 25 minutes or until liquid is absorbed. Yield: 4 to 6 servings.

RICE AND GREEN CHILES

4 cups cooked regular rice
1 (16-ounce) carton commercial sour cream
1 teaspoon salt
¾ cup (3 ounces) shredded Monterey Jack
    cheese
¾ cup (3 ounces) shredded sharp Cheddar
    cheese
1 (4-ounce) can whole green chiles, seeded
    and cut into strips

Combine rice, sour cream, and salt; stir well. Spoon half into a buttered 10- x 6- x 2-inch baking dish. Layer half the cheeses and half the green chiles on top; repeat layers with remaining ingredients. Bake at 350° for 20 minutes or until thoroughly heated and cheese is melted. Yield: 6 to 8 servings.   *Kathryn Watkins,*
Justin, Tex.

SPANISH-STYLE RICE

2 (8-ounce) cans tomato sauce
½ cup water
⅓ cup chopped onion
⅓ cup chopped green pepper
¼ cup butter or margarine
1 teaspoon sugar
½ teaspoon prepared mustard
¼ teaspoon salt
Dash of pepper
6 cups cooked regular rice

Combine first 9 ingredients in a 2½-quart saucepan, stirring well. Bring to a boil; cover and cook 15 minutes. Stir in cooked rice. Remove from heat; cover and let stand 5 minutes. Stir well before serving. Yield: 8 servings.
Elaine Bay,
Point, Tex.

RICE LYONNAISE

2 tablespoons butter or margarine
¾ cup chopped onion
3 cups cooked regular rice
¼ cup chopped pimiento

Melt butter in a heavy skillet; sauté onion until tender. Stir in rice and pimiento; cook, stirring constantly, until thoroughly heated. Yield: 4 to 6 servings.

Mrs. Edward R. Haug,
Sulphur, La.

PIQUANT RUTABAGAS

3 cups peeled and diced rutabaga
2 tablespoons butter or margarine, melted
1 tablespoon light brown sugar
2 tablespoons soy sauce
1 tablespoon lemon juice
1 teaspoon Worcestershire sauce

Cook rutabaga in a small amount of boiling water 20 minutes or until tender; drain. Combine butter, brown sugar, soy sauce, lemon juice, and Worcestershire sauce in a saucepan; heat thoroughly, but do not boil. Pour sauce over rutabaga, and mix gently. Yield: 4 to 6 servings.

SPINACH AU GRATIN

1 pound fresh spinach
4 to 5 slices bacon
2 tablespoons all-purpose flour
1 cup milk
½ cup (2 ounces) shredded Cheddar cheese
½ cup soft breadcrumbs

Wash spinach thoroughly; chop coarsely. Cook with water clinging to leaves in a covered saucepan until just tender.

Cook bacon until crisp, reserving ¼ cup drippings. Return 2 tablespoons bacon drippings to skillet; blend in flour, stirring until smooth. Add milk gradually; cook, stirring constantly, until thickened. Add cheese, stirring until melted.

Combine cooked spinach and cheese sauce; spoon into a greased 1-quart casserole. Crumble bacon over top. Combine breadcrumbs with remaining 2 tablespoons reserved bacon drippings; sprinkle over bacon. Bake at 350° for 20 minutes or until breadcrumbs are browned. Yield: 4 servings.

SPINACH SAUTE

1 pound fresh spinach
1 large tomato, peeled and cut into thin wedges
2 cloves garlic, crushed
2 to 3 tablespoons vegetable oil
Salt and pepper to taste

Wash spinach thoroughly and drain. Sauté tomato and garlic in oil in a large skillet. Add spinach; cover and cook over low heat 15 minutes, stirring once or twice. Add salt and pepper to taste. Cook, uncovered, 5 to 10 minutes longer, stirring occasionally. Yield: 4 servings.

SAUSAGE-STUFFED ACORN SQUASH

2 medium acorn squash
Salt
½ pound bulk sausage
1 small onion, chopped
¾ cup breadcrumbs

Wash squash; cut in half lengthwise and remove seeds. Place squash, cut side down, in a shallow baking dish. Add ½ inch boiling water and bake at 375° for 35 minutes. Turn cut side up and sprinkle with salt; set aside.

Cook sausage and onion until browned, stirring to crumble meat; drain. Stir in breadcrumbs; spoon into squash cavities. Bake at 375° for 20 minutes. Yield: 4 servings.

Pat Stratford,
Burlington, N.C.

APPLE-STUFFED ACORN SQUASH

3 medium acorn squash
¼ cup butter or margarine, melted and divided
Salt
Ground cinnamon
3 apples, peeled, cored, and chopped
1 tablespoon grated lemon rind
1 tablespoon lemon juice
½ cup honey

Wash squash; cut in half lengthwise, and remove seeds. Place squash, cut side down, in a 13- x 9- x 2-inch baking dish; add ½ inch boiling water and bake at 375° for 35 minutes. Turn cut side up, brushing cut surfaces and cavities with 2 tablespoons butter. Sprinkle lightly with salt and cinnamon.

Combine apples, lemon rind and juice, remaining 2 tablespoons butter, and honey; mix well, and spoon into squash cavities. Bake at 350° for 30 minutes. Yield: 6 servings.

Debra S. Petersen,
Slidell, La.

GLAZED ACORN RINGS

1 large acorn squash
⅓ cup orange juice
½ cup firmly packed brown sugar
¼ cup light corn syrup
¼ cup butter or margarine
2 teaspoons grated lemon rind
⅛ teaspoon salt
Orange slices (optional)
Parsley (optional)

Cut squash into ¾-inch slices; remove seeds and membrane. Arrange squash in a lightly greased, shallow baking dish. Pour orange juice over squash. Cover and bake at 350° for 30 minutes.

Combine next 5 ingredients in a saucepan. Bring to a boil; reduce heat, and simmer 5 minutes. Pour sugar mixture over squash. Bake, uncovered, for an additional 15 to 20

minutes or until squash is tender, basting occasionally. Garnish with orange slices and parsley, if desired. Yield: 4 to 6 servings.

CONTINENTAL SQUASH

8 small zucchini, cut into ½-inch slices
¼ cup butter or margarine
2 teaspoons water
1 clove garlic, pressed
½ teaspoon salt
1 teaspoon pepper

Sauté squash in butter in a large skillet 2 to 3 minutes. Add water, garlic, salt, and pepper. Cover and cook over low heat 8 minutes. Yield: 6 to 8 servings.

Mrs. H. J. Sherrer,
Bay City, Tex.

SPINACH-STUFFED ZUCCHINI

3 medium zucchini
Salt
1 (10-ounce) package frozen chopped spinach
2 tablespoons all-purpose flour
½ cup milk
4 slices bacon, cooked, drained, and crumbled
½ cup (2 ounces) shredded Cheddar cheese
Chopped pimiento (optional)

Wash zucchini thoroughly; cut off stem end. Drop zucchini into a small amount of boiling salted water; cover, lower heat, and cook 10 to 12 minutes. Drain, and allow to cool to touch.

Cut zucchini in half lengthwise. Remove pulp, leaving a firm shell; chop pulp. Sprinkle shells with salt to taste; set aside.

Cook spinach according to package directions; drain, and squeeze dry. Combine flour and milk; add zucchini pulp and spinach. Cook over low heat, stirring constantly, until thickened. Spoon spinach mixture into zucchini shells. Sprinkle with bacon and top with cheese.

Place zucchini shells in a shallow baking pan; bake at 350° for 15 to 20 minutes. Garnish with pimiento, if desired. Yield: 6 servings.

ZUCCHINI FRY

1 pound zucchini
Salt and pepper to taste
2 eggs, beaten
About 1 cup cornmeal
Vegetable oil

Wash zucchini, trim ends, and cut into ½-inch slices. Sprinkle with salt and pepper. Dip slices into egg; dredge in cornmeal. Cook over medium heat in ¼-inch oil until golden brown, turning once. Serve hot. Yield: 4 to 6 servings.

Carolyn Beyer,
Fredericksburg, Tex.

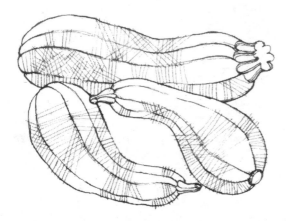

SQUASH MEDLEY

2 tablespoons butter or margarine
1 medium onion, thinly sliced
1 large zucchini, thinly sliced
4 medium-size yellow squash, thinly sliced
1 medium-size green pepper, cut into thin strips
3 medium tomatoes, peeled and quartered
1 teaspoon salt
Dash of pepper
1 cup grated Parmesan cheese

Melt butter in hot wok or large skillet, coating sides and bottom of pan. Add onion; stir-fry briefly. Stir in zucchini, yellow squash, and green pepper; cook 2 to 3 minutes or until crisp-tender. Add tomatoes, salt, and pepper;

stir well. Sprinkle Parmesan cheese over vegetables, and toss mixture gently until cheese melts. Yield: 6 servings.

Mrs. Melvin J. Cheatham,
Gladys, Va.

SQUASH PATTIES

2 cups grated uncooked yellow squash
2 teaspoons grated onion
2 teaspoons sugar
½ teaspoon salt
⅛ teaspoon pepper
¼ cup plus 2 tablespoons all-purpose flour
2 eggs, beaten
2 tablespoons margarine

Combine first 5 ingredients; cover, and let stand 30 minutes. Drain thoroughly. Add flour and eggs; stir well. Melt margarine in a large skillet over medium heat. Drop squash mixture by tablespoonfuls into hot margarine; cook until golden brown, turning once. Yield: 6 to 8 servings.

Annette Hendrix,
Mt. Holly, N.C.

CHEDDAR SQUASH BAKE

2 pounds yellow squash
¼ teaspoon salt
2 eggs, separated
1 (8-ounce) carton commercial sour cream
2 tablespoons all-purpose flour
1½ cups (6 ounces) shredded Cheddar cheese
4 slices bacon, cooked and crumbled
⅓ cup fine, dry breadcrumbs
1 tablespoon butter or margarine, melted

Wash squash thoroughly; trim off ends. Place in boiling salted water to cover. Cook 15 minutes or until crisp-tender. Drain and cool slightly. Thinly slice squash; sprinkle with salt.

Beat egg yolks until thick and lemon colored; stir in sour cream and flour. Beat egg whites (at room temperature) until stiff peaks form; fold into yolk mixture.

Layer half of the squash, egg mixture, and cheese in a lightly greased 12- x 8- x 2-inch baking dish. Sprinkle with bacon. Layer remaining squash, egg mixture, and cheese. Combine breadcrumbs and butter; sprinkle over top. Bake at 350° for 20 to 25 minutes. Yield: 8 to 10 servings.

Carol T. Keith,
Fincastle, Va.

FRIED GREEN TOMATOES

1 egg, slightly beaten
½ cup milk
½ cup cornmeal
¼ cup all-purpose flour
1 teaspoon salt
½ teaspoon pepper
3 medium-size green tomatoes, sliced
Vegetable oil

Combine egg and milk; mix well. Stir together cornmeal, flour, salt, and pepper. Dip tomato slices in egg mixture and dredge in cornmeal mixture. Fry tomato slices in hot oil until browned, turning once. Drain on paper towels. Serve hot. Yield: 4 to 6 servings.

Cathy Breazeale,
Ellisville, Miss.

HERBED TOMATOES

1 (28-ounce) can whole tomatoes, drained
1¼ cups chicken and herb-flavored stuffing
    mix, divided
1 small onion, finely chopped
1½ teaspoons sugar
1 teaspoon salt
¼ teaspoon dried whole oregano
¼ teaspoon dried rosemary
1 tablespoon butter or margarine

Cut tomatoes into quarters, reserving juice. Combine tomatoes, juice, 1 cup stuffing mix, onion, sugar, salt, oregano, and rosemary; mix well. Pour into a greased 1-quart casserole. Sprinkle with remaining stuffing mix, and dot with butter. Bake at 375° for 45 minutes. Yield: 3 to 4 servings.

Mrs. J. W. Craft,
Harlan, Ky.

MARINATED TOMATOES

½ cup vegetable oil
2 tablespoons vinegar
2 tablespoons lemon juice
½ teaspoon salt
¼ teaspoon dry mustard
4 medium tomatoes, cut into ¾-inch slices
1 medium onion, sliced
Parsley

Combine first 5 ingredients in a small mixing bowl, stirring well. Place tomatoes in a medium bowl; add marinade. Top with onion slices and parsley. Cover bowl, and refrigerate overnight. Yield: about 6 to 8 servings.

STUFFED TOMATO SURPRISE

3 slices bacon
¼ cup chopped onion
½ pound fresh spinach, chopped
½ cup commercial sour cream
Dash of hot sauce
4 medium tomatoes
Salt
½ cup (2 ounces) shredded mozzarella cheese

Cook bacon until crisp; drain, reserving 2 tablespoons drippings. Crumble bacon, and set aside.

Sauté onion in reserved bacon drippings until tender; stir in spinach. Cover and cook 3 to 5 minutes or until tender. Remove from heat; stir in sour cream, bacon, and hot sauce.

Cut tops from tomatoes; scoop out pulp, leaving shells intact. Chop pulp, and add to spinach mixture. Drain tomato shells, and sprinkle with salt; fill with vegetable mixture.

Place stuffed tomatoes in an 8-inch square baking dish; bake at 375° for 20 minutes. Top with cheese, and bake an additional 3 minutes or until cheese melts. Yield: 4 servings.

Tip: Wash or chop vegetables and open cans before you begin preparing any recipe. It is also a good idea to have most ingredients measured before beginning to cook.

ZESTY BROILED TOMATOES

2 tablespoons commercial sour cream
2 tablespoons mayonnaise
1 tablespoon grated Parmesan cheese
¼ teaspoon garlic salt
1½ teaspoons lemon juice
¼ teaspoon chopped parsley
1 green onion, chopped
2 to 3 tomatoes, halved

Combine first 7 ingredients; spread a small amount of sour cream mixture on cut side of each tomato half. Broil until lightly browned and bubbly. Yield: 4 to 6 servings.

VEGETABLE MEDLEY SAUTE

2 tablespoons vegetable oil
2 (10-ounce) packages frozen cauliflower, thawed
2 (10-ounce) packages frozen English peas, thawed
2 pimientos, coarsely chopped
½ teaspoon salt
⅛ teaspoon pepper

Heat oil in a heavy skillet. Add cauliflower; cover and cook over low heat 5 minutes, stirring occasionally. Add peas; cover and cook over medium heat 5 minutes, stirring occasionally. Stir in pimiento, salt, and pepper. Yield: 8 servings.

RATATOUILLE

2½ cups thinly sliced onion
2 teaspoons minced garlic
¼ cup vegetable oil
2 pounds eggplant, peeled and cubed
2 pounds zucchini, sliced
3 pounds tomatoes, quartered
½ cup chopped parsley
2 teaspoons dried whole basil
Salt and pepper to taste

Sauté onion and garlic in oil until crisp-tender. Add eggplant, and cook 10 minutes; add zucchini, and cook 5 minutes. Add remaining ingredients. Cover and cook over low heat 30 minutes, stirring frequently. Serve hot or cold. Yield: 8 to 10 servings.

THREE-VEGETABLE CASSEROLE

1 (10-ounce) package frozen English peas in butter sauce
1 (10-ounce) package frozen baby lima beans in butter sauce
1 (16-ounce) can French-style green beans, drained
1 (8-ounce) can sliced water chestnuts, drained
1 cup mayonnaise
1 small onion, chopped
1 tablespoon prepared mustard
1 tablespoon Worcestershire sauce
Salt and pepper to taste
2 tablespoons butter or margarine, melted
1 cup herb-seasoned stuffing mix

Cook peas and limas according to package directions, but do not drain. Combine peas, limas, and remaining ingredients except butter and stuffing mix; stir to combine. Spoon into a lightly greased 2-quart casserole. Combine butter and stuffing mix; sprinkle over vegetables. Bake at 350° for 20 minutes or until bubbly. Yield: 6 to 8 servings.   *Mrs. D. D. Wiltus,*
Ninety Six, S.C.

Cheese-Topped Cauliflower (page 75) and Glazed Acorn Rings (page 83) are two delicious ways to capture the flavor of fall.

Overleaf: *Nothing can be more satisfying on a chilly evening than a steaming bowl of Vegetable Beef Stew (page 93).*

Soups and Stews

CREAM OF JERUSALEM ARTICHOKE SOUP

1 large onion, diced
2 tablespoons butter or margarine, melted and divided
2 cups peeled, cubed Jerusalem artichokes
1 tablespoon all-purpose flour
½ teaspoon salt
⅛ teaspoon ground nutmeg
Pinch of sugar
2 cups water
1 cup evaporated milk
1 egg yolk, slightly beaten

Sauté onion in 1 tablespoon butter 5 minutes in a Dutch oven; add artichoke, and sauté 3 minutes. Stir in flour, salt, nutmeg, and sugar; gradually add water, stirring constantly. Cook over medium heat until artichoke is tender.

Mash artichoke in liquid; add milk, and simmer 5 to 10 minutes. Add remaining butter. Stir a small amount of hot mixture into egg yolk; gradually add to remaining hot mixture, stirring well. Yield: 6 to 8 servings.

Tip: Use a bulb baster to remove fat from broth, stew, or soup.

CREAM OF ZUCCHINI SOUP

3 pounds zucchini, cut into 2-inch slices
1 (10½-ounce) can beef broth, undiluted
2 cups water
½ cup chopped onion or 1 tablespoon instant minced onion
1½ teaspoons salt
⅛ teaspoon garlic powder
4 cups milk or half-and-half
Grated Parmesan cheese
Cooked and crumbled bacon

Combine first 6 ingredients in a large Dutch oven; cook over medium heat until vegetables are tender. Place zucchini mixture, 2 cups at a time, in container of electric blender; blend until smooth.

Return puree to Dutch oven; add milk and cook over low heat until thoroughly heated, stirring occasionally. Top with Parmesan cheese and bacon. Yield: about 12 cups.

Note: Soup base freezes well. Omit milk, cheese, and bacon. Pour zucchini puree into 1-pint freezer containers, leaving ¾-inch headspace; freeze. At serving time, thaw zucchini puree; add 1 cup milk for each pint of soup base and proceed as directed. Allow 1 pint of base for 4 servings. *Mrs. Otis Jackson, Wedowee, Ala.*

PEANUT SOUP

1 medium onion, minced
1 cup sliced celery
½ cup butter or margarine
2 tablespoons all-purpose flour
2 quarts chicken broth
1 cup creamy peanut butter
1 cup half-and-half
¼ cup chopped parsley
¼ cup chopped salted peanuts

Sauté onion and celery in butter until tender. Stir in flour, blending well. Stir in chicken broth; cook, stirring frequently, until mixture comes to a boil. Reduce heat to simmer; stir in peanut butter and half-and-half. Simmer 5 to 10 minutes. Top with parsley and peanuts before serving. Yield: about 10 servings.

GARDEN HARVEST CHOWDER

4 slices bacon
2 tablespoons sliced green onion
½ cup chopped celery
½ cup peeled and thinly sliced carrot
2 cups mashed potatoes
1 (17-ounce) can cream-style corn
½ cup frozen English peas
2 cups milk
½ teaspoon salt
1 cup (4 ounces) shredded Cheddar cheese
1 large tomato, peeled and thinly sliced
Seasoned pepper

Fry bacon in a large saucepan until crisp; drain on paper towels. Crumble bacon. Reserve 1 tablespoon drippings in pan.

Sauté onion, celery, and carrot in reserved drippings for 2 minutes. Stir in potatoes, corn, peas, milk, salt, and cheese. Cook over medium heat, stirring occasionally, until cheese melts.

Top each serving with a tomato slice, bacon, and a dash of seasoned pepper. Yield: about 7 cups. *Ella Stanley, Coeburn, Va.*

VEGETABLE-BEAN SOUP

1 cup dried navy beans
8 cups water
3 carrots, peeled and diced
2 stalks celery, chopped
3 medium tomatoes, peeled and chopped
3 small onions, minced
2 cloves garlic, minced
3 tablespoons olive oil
Pinch of savory
1 teaspoon salt

Wash beans thoroughly; place in a large Dutch oven. Add water; bring to a boil. Remove from heat; cover and let stand for 1 hour. Return water to a boil; reduce heat, and simmer 45 minutes.

Add remaining ingredients; simmer, uncovered, about 30 minutes or until beans are tender. Yield: 8 cups. *Betty Collier, Fern Creek, Ky.*

BEEFY BARLEY SOUP

2 pounds cross-cut beef shanks or shoulder roast
1 tablespoon vegetable oil
1 soupbone
2 quarts water
¼ cup chopped celery
2 tablespoons chopped parsley
¼ teaspoon dried whole thyme
1 bay leaf
2 teaspoons salt
2 teaspoons Worcestershire sauce
½ cup sliced fresh mushrooms
2 potatoes, diced
2 carrots, diced
1 cup pearl barley
3 tablespoons butter
Salt and pepper to taste
3 tablespoons commercial sour cream
Fresh parsley (optional)

Brown beef in hot oil in a Dutch oven; add soupbone, water, celery, seasonings, and Worcestershire sauce. Cover and bring to a boil. Reduce heat, and simmer 2 hours.

Remove soupbone and meat from Dutch oven; trim meat from bones. Dice meat, and set aside; discard bones. Strain broth, and skim off excess fat. Return meat and broth to Dutch oven; add remaining ingredients except sour cream and parsley. Bring to a boil, and simmer 45 minutes. Stir in sour cream. Garnish with parsley, if desired. Yield: 8 servings.

COUNTRY VEGETABLE GOULASH

1 pound ground beef
Dash of Worcestershire sauce
1 medium onion, chopped
2 cups cubed potatoes
5 cups water
1 to 1½ cups peeled and chopped carrot
3 to 4 medium tomatoes, peeled and cubed
¼ cup catsup
2 beef-flavored bouillon cubes
½ to 1 cup canned or frozen English peas
½ to 1 cup frozen baby butter beans
½ to 1 cup fresh or frozen cut green beans
½ to 1 cup frozen sliced okra
½ to 1 cup canned whole kernel corn (optional)
Pinch of dried whole thyme
Pinch of dried whole basil
1 small bay leaf
1 teaspoon salt
¼ teaspoon pepper
1 teaspoon sugar

Combine ground beef and Worcestershire sauce in a large Dutch oven; cook over medium heat until meat is browned, stirring to crumble. Drain well. Add remaining ingredients. Cover, and simmer 45 minutes or until vegetables are tender. Yield: about 11 cups.
Mrs. Dan Wagner,
Jackson, Miss.

HAM-VEGETABLE CHOWDER

3 cups water
4 medium potatoes, cubed
1 cup sliced celery
1 cup sliced carrot
½ cup diced onion
2 teaspoons salt
¼ teaspoon pepper
½ cup butter or margarine
½ cup all-purpose flour
4 cups milk
4 cups (16 ounces) shredded sharp Cheddar cheese
2 cups cubed cooked ham
Hot sauce

Bring water to a boil in a Dutch oven; add vegetables, salt, and pepper. Cover and simmer 10 minutes or until vegetables are done.

Melt butter in a large saucepan over low heat; add flour, stirring until smooth. Cook 1 minute stirring constantly. Gradually add milk; cook over medium heat, stirring constantly, until thickened and bubbly. Add cheese and stir until melted.

Stir cheese mixture into vegetables. Add ham and hot sauce to taste, stirring well. Heat thoroughly, but do not boil. Yield: 12 servings.

VENISON SOUP

2 meaty venison bones (rib, neck, or hindquarter)
4½ to 5 cups water
1¼ teaspoons salt, divided
2 eggs, beaten
Dash of pepper
Dash of ground nutmeg
3 tablespoons chopped parsley

Place bones, water, and 1 teaspoon salt in a large Dutch oven. Bring to a boil; reduce heat, and simmer 1½ to 2 hours. Remove bones; strain liquid. Return broth to Dutch oven; bring to simmer. Combine remaining ingredients; gradually pour into broth, stirring constantly. Yield: about 4 cups.

MEXICAN SOUP

1 pound ground beef
1 medium onion, chopped
4 medium potatoes, cubed
2½ cups water, divided
1 (16-ounce) can stewed tomatoes, undrained
2 teaspoons ground cumin
2 teaspoons chili powder
¼ teaspoon garlic salt
1 teaspoon salt
⅛ teaspoon pepper

Cook ground beef and onion until meat is browned, stirring to crumble meat; drain well.

Combine potatoes and 1½ cups water in a large Dutch oven; bring to a boil. Reduce heat; cover, and simmer 15 minutes. Add tomatoes, remaining water, and seasonings; bring to a boil. Add meat mixture; reduce heat, cover and simmer 45 minutes. Yield: 7 cups.

Toddie Lee Burns,
Canton, Tex.

CHILI

5 pounds ground beef
6 (16-ounce) cans kidney beans
4 medium onions, chopped
⅓ to ½ cup chili powder
6 bay leaves
½ (2-ounce) bottle hot sauce
6 chili peppers, chopped
1 (14-ounce) bottle catsup
⅔ cup steak sauce
¼ cup Worcestershire sauce
Dash of garlic powder
Dash of onion salt
2 (6-ounce) cans tomato paste
2 (16-ounce) cans tomatoes, undrained
Salt and pepper to taste
Tomato juice (optional)

Cook ground beef in a Dutch oven over medium heat until browned, stirring to crumble meat; drain well. Add enough water to cover.

Add remaining ingredients except tomato juice. Cover and simmer over low heat about 2 hours, stirring frequently. If additional liquid is needed, add tomato juice. Yield: 15 to 18 servings.

CORNED BEEF-VEGETABLE STEW

1 (46-ounce) can tomato juice
1 (17-ounce) can English peas, undrained
1 (17-ounce) can cream-style corn
1 (12-ounce) can corned beef, chopped
1 cup water
Salt and pepper to taste
½ to 1 cup uncooked elbow macaroni

Combine all ingredients except macaroni in a Dutch oven; bring to a boil, and simmer 20 minutes. Add macaroni; simmer 8 to 10 minutes or until macaroni is just tender, stirring occasionally. Yield: 8 to 10 servings.

COWBOY STEW

1½ pounds ground beef
1 medium onion, chopped
½ teaspoon salt
Dash of pepper
4 medium potatoes, peeled and cubed
2 cups water
1 (16-ounce) can whole tomatoes, undrained
1 (15-ounce) can ranch-style beans, undrained
1 (12-ounce) can whole kernel corn, undrained
1 (10¾-ounce) can tomato soup, undiluted
1 (4-ounce) can chopped green chiles

Combine beef, onion, salt, and pepper in a large Dutch oven; cook over medium heat until meat is browned, stirring to crumble; drain.

Add potatoes and water to meat mixture; cover and cook over medium heat until potatoes are tender. Add remaining ingredients; cover and simmer 1 hour, stirring occasionally. Yield: 6 to 8 servings.

Mary K. Owings,
Sentinel, Okla.

CHUNKY BEEF STEW

1½ pounds lean boneless beef, cut into 1-inch cubes
2 tablespoons vegetable oil
4 cups water
1 cup catsup
3 medium potatoes, peeled and cubed
1 large onion, diced
3 medium carrots, peeled and sliced
1 teaspoon Worcestershire sauce
¼ teaspoon salt
¼ teaspoon garlic salt
¼ teaspoon curry powder
⅛ teaspoon celery salt
⅛ teaspoon pepper
1 (17-ounce) can English peas, drained

Cook beef in hot oil in a large Dutch oven until browned. Add remaining ingredients, except peas. Bring to a boil; cover, reduce heat, and simmer 1½ to 2 hours, stirring occasionally. Stir in peas, and cook an additional 10 minutes. Yield: 6 to 8 servings.
Gladys Cardill,
Green Mountain, N.C.

VEGETABLE BEEF STEW

1 pound lean boneless beef, cut into 1-inch cubes
2 tablespoons vegetable oil
2 cups water
2 cups tomato juice
2 medium onions, chopped
1 (16-ounce) can whole tomatoes, undrained
1 (8¾-ounce) can whole kernel corn, undrained
1 cup peeled and cubed potatoes
1 cup peeled and sliced carrot
1 cup chopped celery
1 cup frozen English peas
1 cup frozen lima beans
1 tablespoon sugar
2 teaspoons salt
2 teaspoons pepper
1 teaspoon hot sauce

Cook beef in hot oil in a large Dutch oven until browned. Add remaining ingredients. Bring to a boil; cover, reduce heat, and simmer 2 to 2½ hours, stirring occasionally. Add additional water during cooking, if necessary. Yield: 6 to 8 servings.
Linda Lawson,
Salem, Va.

OLD-TIME BEEF STEW

2 pounds boneless chuck, cut into 1½-inch cubes
2 tablespoons vegetable oil
1 medium onion, sliced
1 clove garlic
2 cups water
1 tablespoon salt
½ teaspoon pepper
1 teaspoon sugar
1 teaspoon Worcestershire sauce
1 teaspoon soy sauce
1 tablespoon vinegar
1 tablespoon lemon juice
½ teaspoon paprika
1 large bay leaf
1 teaspoon Italian seasoning
Dash of allspice
6 carrots, peeled and sliced
1 pound small white onions, peeled
6 medium potatoes, peeled and cubed
¼ cup cold water
2 tablespoons all-purpose flour

Cook beef in oil in a Dutch oven over medium heat about 20 minutes, turning often to brown evenly. Stir in the next 14 ingredients. Cover and simmer about 1½ hours, stirring occasionally.

Remove bay leaf and garlic. Add vegetables; cover and simmer 30 minutes or until vegetables are done. Combine ¼ cup cold water and flour in a small mixing bowl, mixing well; pour into stew, stirring constantly until gravy thickens. Simmer 5 minutes. Yield: 6 to 8 servings.
E. Gayle Pace,
Raleigh, N.C.

CHUCKWAGON STEW

¼ cup all-purpose flour
2 teaspoons salt, divided
½ teaspoon pepper, divided
1½ pounds round steak, cut into bite-size
   pieces
2 tablespoons vegetable oil
1 (28-ounce) can tomatoes, undrained
1 medium onion, coarsely chopped
1 clove garlic, minced
1 tablespoon Worcestershire sauce
½ teaspoon dried whole basil
2 (10-ounce) packages frozen mixed vegetables
½ cup butter or margarine
3 medium potatoes, peeled and cut into 1-inch
   cubes

Combine flour, 1 teaspoon salt, and ¼ teaspoon pepper; coat steak well with flour mixture. Reserve any leftover flour. Brown meat in oil in a large Dutch oven. Add tomatoes, reserved flour, onion, garlic, Worcestershire sauce, basil, remaining 1 teaspoon salt, and ¼ teaspoon pepper. Bring to a boil; reduce heat and simmer 45 minutes, stirring occasionally. Add vegetables, butter, and potatoes. Simmer 1 hour. Yield: 6 to 8 servings.

Mrs. Ray Bosserman,
Staunton, Va.

CREAMY BEEF STEW

½ (10¾-ounce) can cream of mushroom soup,
   undiluted
½ cup milk
2 tablespoons butter or margarine
1 pound lean boneless beef, cut into
   1-inch cubes
2 large onions, sliced
3 small potatoes, peeled and sliced
1 (8-ounce) carton commercial sour cream
¼ cup (1 ounce) shredded Cheddar cheese
   (optional)

Combine soup and milk; mix until smooth and set aside. Melt butter in a large skillet; add beef and cook over medium heat until browned,

stirring occasionally. Add onion, potatoes, and soup mixture; cover and cook over low heat about 1 hour, stirring occasionally.

Stir in sour cream and cook just until thoroughly heated. Garnish with cheese, if desired. Yield: about 4 servings.

Dorothy L. Anderson,
Manor, Tex.

BRUNSWICK STEW

1 (4½-pound) pork roast
1 (4½-pound) hen
3 (16-ounce) cans chopped tomatoes,
   undrained
1 (8-ounce) can tomato sauce
3 large onions, finely chopped
2 small green peppers, finely chopped
¾ cup vinegar
¼ cup sugar
1 cup water
¼ cup all-purpose flour
1 tablespoon salt
½ teaspoon pepper
½ teaspoon ground turmeric
2 to 3 tablespoons hot sauce
1 (20-ounce) package frozen shoepeg corn

Place roast, fat side up, on rack in a roasting pan. Insert meat thermometer, making sure it does not touch bone or fat. Bake at 325° until thermometer reaches 170°. Cool. Trim and discard fat; cut pork into 2-inch pieces.

Place hen in a Dutch oven, and cover with water. Bring to a boil; cover and reduce heat. Simmer 2 hours or until tender. Remove hen from broth and cool. (Reserve broth for use in another recipe.) Bone hen, and cut meat into 2-inch pieces.

Grind pork and chicken coarsely in food processor or with meat grinder. Combine ground meat and next 6 ingredients in a large Dutch oven. Combine water and flour, stirring until flour is dissolved. Stir into meat mixture. Stir in salt, pepper, turmeric, and hot sauce. Cook over medium heat about 30 minutes, stirring occasionally. Add water, as needed, to reach desired consistency. Stir in corn, and cook an additional 10 minutes. Yield: 14 to 16 servings.

HEARTY STEW

4 cups cubed cooked meat (beef, veal, or lamb)
4 medium potatoes, cooked and cubed
1½ cups carrot, sliced and cooked
¾ cup English peas
1½ cups green beans
½ cup green pepper, chopped
¾ cup cream-style corn
¼ cup onion, chopped
½ teaspoon salt
2 tablespoons chili powder
¼ cup all-purpose flour
1 cup water
¾ cup tomato juice

Combine meat and vegetables in a Dutch oven, stirring to mix well. Combine remaining ingredients in a jar; shake vigorously. Add to meat mixture and simmer 30 to 45 minutes. Yield: 8 to 10 servings.   *Carolyn Beyer, Fredericksburg, Tex.*

LAMB STEW

2 pounds boneless, cubed lamb
1 tablespoon vegetable oil
4 to 5 cups hot water
1 stalk celery with leaves, chopped
1 onion, sliced
½ cup uncooked barley
2 tablespoons chopped parsley
2 teaspoons salt
6 potatoes, peeled and cut into 1-inch cubes

Brown lamb in oil in a large Dutch oven; add 4 cups water, celery, onion, barley, parsley, and salt. Cover and simmer 1½ hours. Add potatoes and continue cooking 30 minutes, adding more water if needed. Yield: 8 servings.
Mable A. Collins, Frankfort, Ky.

CHICKEN STEW

1 (5-pound) hen
½ cup chopped celery
1 tablespoon salt
1 (46-ounce) can tomato juice
2 potatoes, diced
1 large onion, chopped
1 (17-ounce) can cream-style corn
1 (6-ounce) jar prepared mustard
1 tablespoon Worcestershire sauce
Salt and pepper to taste

Place hen in a Dutch oven and cover with water. Add celery and 1 tablespoon salt; cover and cook over medium heat until hen is very tender (about 3 hours). Cool.

Remove skin and bones from hen; cut meat into bite-size pieces, and return to broth. Add remaining ingredients to broth. Bring to a boil; reduce heat, and simmer about 30 minutes or until potatoes and onion are tender. Yield: 8 to 10 servings.

CREOLE FISH STEW

1 cup chopped onion
½ cup chopped green pepper
¼ cup butter or margarine
1 (16-ounce) can chopped tomatoes, undrained
1½ teaspoons garlic salt
1 teaspoon whole thyme
½ teaspoon red pepper
1 (10-ounce) package frozen succotash
2 (12-ounce) packages frozen cod fillets, thawed and cut into 3-inch pieces
½ teaspoon salt

Sauté onion and green pepper in butter about 5 minutes or until tender; stir in tomatoes, garlic salt, thyme, and red pepper. Simmer over low heat 5 minutes, stirring mixture frequently. Add succotash, fish, and salt; cover and simmer 15 minutes or until fish flakes easily when tested with a fork. Yield: 6 servings.

OYSTER STEW

1 quart half-and-half or milk
2 tablespoons butter or margarine
2 green onions, chopped
1 pint oysters, undrained
Salt and red pepper to taste

Heat half-and-half in top of a double boiler until hot but not boiling. Melt butter in a saucepan over medium heat; add onion, and sauté lightly. Add oysters, and cook until edges begin to curl. Combine oyster mixture with half-and-half; stir in salt and red pepper. Serve with crackers. Yield: 6 to 8 servings.

CHICKEN-OYSTER GUMBO

1 (2½- to 3-pound) chicken, cut up
Salt
Red and black pepper
½ cup vegetable oil
½ cup all-purpose flour
1 large onion, chopped
2 quarts hot water
1 to 2 pints oysters, undrained
2 stalks celery, chopped
½ green pepper, chopped
½ cup chopped parsley
½ cup chopped green onion tops
Hot cooked rice
Gumbo filé (optional)

Season chicken with salt and pepper. Heat oil in a heavy iron pot; add chicken, and cook until browned. Remove chicken, and stir flour into oil; cook over medium heat until a dark roux is formed, stirring constantly. Add onion to roux, and cook until tender, stirring constantly; add chicken. Gradually stir in hot water, blending well. Bring to a boil, and simmer about 1 hour. Remove chicken bones, if desired. Season to taste with salt and pepper. Add oysters, celery, green pepper, parsley, and green onion to gumbo; simmer 20 minutes. Serve over rice. Thicken with gumbo filé, if desired. Yield: 8 to 10 servings.

TURKEY AND SAUSAGE GUMBO

1 turkey carcass
½ cup vegetable oil
½ cup all-purpose flour
2 medium onions, chopped
½ green pepper, chopped
1 stalk celery, chopped
1½ pounds smoked sausage, cut into 2½-inch pieces
Salt
Red and black pepper
¼ cup chopped parsley
¼ cup chopped green onion tops
Hot cooked rice
Gumbo filé (optional)

Use a turkey carcass with a little meat left on it; a smoked turkey is best. Cover carcass with water, and boil until meat leaves bones (about 1 hour). Reserve broth, and remove meat from carcass; discard bones.

Combine oil and flour in a large Dutch oven; cook over medium heat, stirring constantly, until a medium roux is formed. Add onion, green pepper, and celery; cook about 5 minutes or until tender, stirring constantly. Add sausage, turkey, and 2 to 3 quarts broth (add enough water to make 2 quarts, if necessary); simmer 1 hour.

Season gumbo to taste with salt and pepper. Stir in parsley and green onion; cook 10 minutes longer. Serve over rice. Thicken with gumbo filé, if desired. Yield: 8 to 10 servings.

Combine fresh green beans with a variety of vegetables and meats to make tasty soups and stews. Recipes begin on page 89.

Overleaf: *Make the most of your vegetable crop with Chili Sauce (page 103), Cucumber Sandwich Pickles (page 101), Corn Relish (page 103), and Mixed Pickles (page 102).*

Pickling

Pickling is one of the oldest methods of preserving foods. The process involves preserving fruits and vegetables in a vinegar solution to which large amounts of sugar or salt have been added. The name of the pickle is determined by the predominant spice, such as dill pickles and mustard pickles.

Pickles are usually made by two general methods: brined and fresh-pack. Brined pickles, also called fermented or long-process pickles, are soaked in a brine for at least two weeks. After removing the salt from the cured product, vinegar, sugar, and spices are added. Dilled cucumbers and sauerkraut go through this process.

Fresh-pack, or quick-process, pickles are soaked in a brine overnight or in ice water for a few hours. Included in this category are fruit pickles, which are made from whole fruits simmered in vinegar, sugar, and spices; and relishes, which are made from chopped fruits and vegetables simmered in a spiced vinegar.

Essentials for Good Pickles

Ingredients: Only fresh, firm, unbruised fruits and vegetables should be used. Immature or slightly underripe produce makes the best pickles.

A high-grade cider or white distilled vinegar of 4% to 6% acidity should be used in pickling. Do not use vinegars of unknown acidity, and do not dilute vinegar unless instructed to do so. Cider vinegar is preferred for fruit pickles, while others can be made with white distilled vinegar.

Pure granulated pickling salt should be used. Do not use iodized table salt as it could cause the pickles to turn dark. Uniodized table salt may be used, but it may make the brine dark and cloudy.

Spices should be fresh; if they have been stored several years, they have probably lost their flavor.

Use soft water for making brine. Hard water should be boiled 15 minutes and allowed to stand 24 hours before using. Remove any scum on the top, and ladle water out without disturbing any sediment on the bottom. Before using boiled water, add 1 tablespoon vinegar to each gallon.

General Pickling Instructions

Equipment: Pickling liquids should be heated in enamel, stainless steel, aluminum, or glass containers. Do not use iron, copper, brass, or zinc containers or utensils as they may cause undesirable taste and color in pickles.

Glass or stoneware containers should be used for soaking pickles in brine. Use standard canning jars and lids that have been sterilized. You'll also need a water-bath canner with a rack for processing pickles.

Packing and Sealing: Pack pickles and relishes in sterilized jars according to recipe. Eliminate any air bubbles that have formed by running a knife along the inside edge of the jar. Wipe off rim of jars, and seal with new, sterilized lids.

Place jars on rack in water-bath canner filled with actively boiling water, making sure water comes 1 or 2 inches above jar tops. Cover canner, and begin timing when water in canner returns to a full boil. (Add 1 minute of processing time for each 1,000 feet above sea level.)

Cooling and Storing: When processing time is completed, remove jars from canner, and place on a rack or folded towel to cool. Jars should be several inches apart to allow air to circulate around them. After jars have cooled, check lids for seals. (Sealed lids will be indented in the center.) If any jars did not seal, reprocess those jars immediately or refrigerate and use as soon as possible.

To keep pickles at their best, store them in a cool, dark, dry place.

Causes of Pickling Problems

Shriveled pickles may be caused by too strong a vinegar, sugar, or salt solution at the start of the pickling process. If making very sweet or very sour pickles, start with a diluted solution and increase strength gradually. Overcooking or overprocessing may also cause shriveling.

Hollow pickles usually result from poorly developed cucumbers, holding cucumbers too long before pickling, too rapid fermentation (caused by high temperatures), or too strong or too weak a brine during fermentation.

Soft or slippery pickles result from a spoilage condition caused by having too weak a brine, not covering pickles with brine, or not removing scum as it forms.

Dark pickles may be caused by use of iron utensils, ground spices, too much spice, iodized salt, overcooking, or minerals in the water.

BREAD AND BUTTER PICKLES

4 quarts medium cucumbers
6 medium-size white onions, sliced
2 green peppers, chopped
3 cloves garlic
1⅓ cups pickling salt
Crushed ice
5 cups sugar
3 cups vinegar (5% acidity)
1½ teaspoons turmeric
1½ teaspoons celery seeds
2 tablespoons mustard seeds

Wash cucumbers and slice thin. Combine cucumber, onion, green pepper, garlic, and salt in a large Dutch oven. Cover with crushed ice; mix thoroughly and let stand 3 hours. Drain.

Combine remaining ingredients and pour over cucumber mixture. Heat thoroughly, just until boiling. Pack while hot into sterilized pint jars, leaving ½-inch headspace. Cover at once with metal lids, and screw bands tight. Process in boiling-water bath for 5 minutes. Yield: 8 pints.

Virginia Outhouse,
Tavares, Fla.

CRISP CUCUMBER PICKLES

7 pounds small cucumbers
2 gallons ice water
5 pints vinegar (5% acidity)
5 pounds sugar
1 teaspoon ground cinnamon
1 teaspoon ground cloves
1 teaspoon ground allspice
1 teaspoon celery seeds

Wash cucumbers and slice into ⅛-inch-thick slices. Combine cucumber slices and ice water; soak overnight in refrigerator. Drain cucumber slices and rinse in cold water several times. Drain again.

Combine vinegar, sugar, and spices in a Dutch oven; bring to a boil, and pour over cucumber slices. Let stand overnight.

Bring cucumber and syrup mixture to a boil; reduce heat and simmer 1 hour. Pack into hot sterilized jars, leaving ½-inch headspace. Cover at once with metal lids, and screw bands tight. Process in boiling-water bath for 5 minutes. Yield: about 8 pints. *Virginia Outhouse, Tavares, Fla.*

CUCUMBER SANDWICH PICKLES

½ cup pickling salt
6 cups sliced medium cucumbers (¼-inch slices)
3 quarts water, divided
5 cups vinegar (5% acidity), divided
1 cup firmly packed brown sugar
1 cup sugar
½ teaspoon celery seeds
½ teaspoon mustard seeds
½ teaspoon ground turmeric

Sprinkle salt over cucumbers in a large Dutch oven; add 2 quarts water. Cover and let stand 2 to 3 hours. Drain well.

Combine 3 cups vinegar and 3 cups water in a large Dutch oven; bring to a boil. Add cucumbers and simmer about 8 minutes. (Do not allow cucumbers to become soft.) Drain well.

Combine 2 cups vinegar and 1 cup water in a large Dutch oven; add remaining ingredients, except cucumbers. Simmer 10 minutes; add cucumbers. Bring to a boil. Pack into hot sterilized jars, leaving ¼-inch headspace. Cover at once with metal lids, and screw bands tight. Process in boiling-water bath for 10 minutes. Yield: about 3 pints.

BEET PICKLES

8 quarts beets
10 (2-inch) cinnamon sticks
1 tablespoon whole cloves
1½ cups sugar
1 quart vinegar (5% acidity)
1 cup water

Wash and drain beets. Leave roots and about 1 inch of stem at tops. Cover with boiling water and cook until tender. Peel and remove stems and roots.

Tie spices in a cheesecloth bag. Combine spices, sugar, vinegar, and water in a Dutch oven; bring to a boil. Add beets; gently boil 5 minutes. Remove spice bag. Place beets into hot sterilized jars, leaving ½-inch headspace. Process in boiling-water bath for 30 minutes. Yield: about 8 quarts. *Mrs. Jamie L. Sego, Cloverdale, Ala.*

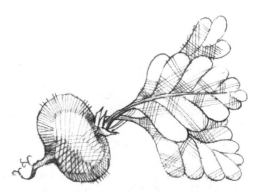

PICKLED OKRA

4 to 4½ pounds small okra pods
7 cloves garlic
7 hot peppers
7 teaspoons dillseeds
4 cups vinegar (5% acidity)
1 cup water
½ cup pickling salt

Wash okra well; drain and set aside. Place 1 clove garlic and 1 hot pepper into each of 7 hot, sterilized pint jars. Pack jars firmly with okra, leaving ½-inch headspace; add 1 teaspoon dillseeds to each.

Combine vinegar, water, and salt in a large saucepan; bring to a boil. Pour over okra, leaving ¼-inch headspace. Cover at once with metal lids, and screw bands tight. Process in boiling-water bath for 10 minutes. Let pickles stand at least 5 weeks before opening. Yield: 7 pints. *Mrs. S. G. Fuzzell, Sr., Brent, Ala.*

MIXED PICKLES

1 cup pickling salt
4 quarts cold water
4 cups sliced small cucumber (1-inch slices)
2 cups sliced carrot (1½-inch slices)
2 cups sliced celery (1½-inch slices)
2 cups small boiling onions
2 sweet red peppers, cut into ½-inch strips
1 small cauliflower, broken into flowerets
6½ cups vinegar (5% acidity)
2 cups sugar
1 fresh hot red pepper, sliced crosswise
¼ cup mustard seeds
2 tablespoons celery seeds

Dissolve salt in water; pour over vegetables in a large crock or plastic container. Cover and allow to stand in a cool place 12 to 18 hours. Drain well.

Combine vinegar, sugar, hot red pepper, mustard seeds, and celery seeds in a 10-quart Dutch oven; bring to a boil and cook 3 minutes. Add vegetables; reduce heat, and simmer until thoroughly heated.

Pack into hot sterilized jars, leaving ¼-inch headspace. Cover at once with metal lids, and screw bands tight. Process in boiling-water bath for 15 minutes. Yield: about 6 pints.

SQUASH PICKLES

3 cups sliced small yellow squash
3 cups sugar
2 cups vinegar (5% acidity)
2 teaspoons mustard seeds
2 teaspoons celery seeds
2 cups coarsely chopped green pepper
2 cups coarsely chopped sweet red pepper
2 large onions, thinly sliced and separated
    into rings

Place squash in salted water to cover, and let stand 1 hour. Drain well and set aside.

Combine sugar, vinegar, mustard seeds, and celery seeds in a large Dutch oven; bring to a boil and add remaining ingredients. Boil

gently 5 minutes. Pack into hot sterilized jars, leaving ½-inch headspace. Cover at once with metal lids, and screw bands tight. Process in boiling-water bath for 15 minutes. Yield: about 5 half-pints.

Fay Crow,
Clinton, Ark.

ZUCCHINI PICKLES

2 quarts (¼-inch-thick slices) zucchini
3 cups thinly sliced onion
3 cups sliced green pepper
1½ quarts cold water
2½ cups vinegar (5% acidity)
2 cups sugar
¾ cup water
½ teaspoon pickling salt
½ teaspoon ground turmeric
1 teaspoon celery seeds
1 teaspoon mustard seeds

Combine zucchini, onion, green pepper, and 1½ quarts cold water in a large bowl; let stand 3 hours. Drain well and set aside.

Combine remaining ingredients in a large Dutch oven, mixing well; bring to a boil and cook 3 minutes. Add vegetables; return to a boil and cook gently 15 to 20 minutes, stirring often. Pack into hot sterilized jars, leaving ½-inch headspace. Cover at once with metal lids, and screw bands tight. Process in boiling-water bath for 10 minutes. Yield: about 3½ pints.

Dean Barrick,
Fort Towson, Okla.

WATERMELON RIND PICKLES

1 large watermelon
1 gallon cold water
1 quart cider vinegar (5% acidity)
8 cups sugar
1 teaspoon mixed pickling spices

Select a melon that has a thick rind. Remove outer green skin and pink flesh; use only the greenish-white parts of the rind. Cut rind into 1-inch cubes. Combine rind and cold water; soak overnight in refrigerator.

Drain; cover with water and boil 30 minutes. Drain.

Combine vinegar, sugar, and pickling spices; cover cubes with this mixture. Boil slowly until cubes look clear (about 1 hour), being sure cubes are covered with syrup throughout cooking. Add water if syrup cooks down.

Pack into hot sterilized jars; cover with syrup, leaving ¼-inch headspace. Cover at once with metal lids and screw bands tight. Process in boiling-water bath for 10 minutes. Yield: about 7 pints.

CORN RELISH

About 18 ears fresh corn
7 quarts water
1 small head cabbage, chopped
1 cup chopped onion
1 cup chopped green pepper
1 cup chopped sweet red pepper
1 to 2 cups sugar
2 tablespoons dry mustard
1 tablespoon celery seeds
1 tablespoon mustard seeds
1 tablespoon salt
1 tablespoon ground turmeric
1 quart vinegar (5% acidity)
1 cup water

Remove husks and silks from corn just before cooking. Bring 7 quarts water to a boil; add corn. Bring water to a second boil; boil 5 minutes. Cut corn from cob, measuring about 2 quarts of kernels.

Combine corn kernels and remaining ingredients in a large saucepan; simmer over low heat 20 minutes. Bring mixture to a boil. Pack into hot sterilized jars, leaving ¼-inch headspace. Cover at once with metal lids, and screw bands tight. Process in boiling-water bath 15 minutes. Yield: about 6 pints.

CHILI SAUCE

4 quarts peeled, cored, and chopped ripe
   tomatoes
2 cups chopped onion
2 cups chopped sweet red pepper
1 fresh hot red pepper, minced
1 cup sugar
3 tablespoons pickling salt
3 tablespoons mixed pickling spices
1 tablespoon celery seeds
1 tablespoon mustard seeds
2½ cups vinegar (5% acidity)

Combine first 6 ingredients in a heavy 10-quart Dutch oven. Simmer, uncovered, 45 minutes.

Tie pickling spices, celery and mustard seeds in a cheesecloth bag; add to tomato mixture. Simmer, uncovered, about 1½ hours or until thickened. Stir in vinegar, and simmer 1 additional hour or until mixture reaches desired thickness. Remove spice bag.

Pour chili sauce into hot sterilized jars, leaving ¼-inch headspace. Cover at once with metal lids, and screw bands tight. Process in boiling-water bath for 15 minutes. Yield: about 4 pints.

Tip: Properly canned foods have been sterilized and won't spoil as long as the container remains airtight. However, most canned foods have a "shelf life" of approximately one year—they then may begin to slowly lose flavor and nutrients. If you use large amounts of canned foods, date them at time of purchase and use the oldest first.

CUCUMBER RELISH

1 gallon finely chopped cucumber
1 quart finely chopped onion
1 cup finely chopped sweet red pepper
1 cup finely chopped green pepper
1 cup finely chopped carrot
3 tablespoons pickling salt
2 teaspoons ground turmeric
1 teaspoon celery seeds
1 teaspoon whole cloves
2 tablespoons mustard seeds
3 (2-inch) cinnamon sticks
3 cups vinegar (5% acidity)
3 cups sugar

Combine first 6 ingredients in a large mixing bowl; stir well, and refrigerate at least 8 hours or overnight. Drain.

Tie spices in a cheesecloth bag. Combine spice bag, vinegar, and sugar in a Dutch oven; bring to a boil. Add vegetables; boil gently, stirring often, for 15 to 20 mintues or until of desired consistency. Pack into hot sterilized jars, leaving ½-inch headspace. Cover at once with metal lids, and screw bands tight. Process in boiling-water bath for 15 minutes. Yield: about 6 pints.   *Mrs. Ansel L. Todd,*
Royston, Ga.

Preserving

Jams, jellies, preserves, conserves, and marmalades are a delightful way to enjoy summer fruits year-round. The main ingredients of all these products are fruit and sugar, usually concentrated by some method of cooking.

Jams are made from crushed fruit with sugar added; the mixture is then cooked to a thick, even consistency.

Jellies are made from fruit juice; sugar and possibly a liquid or powdered pectin are added to make the product firm enough to hold its shape, yet soft enough to spread.

Conserves are jamlike products made from a mixture of fruits, usually including citrus fruits; nuts and raisins are sometimes added.

Marmalade is a tender jelly with very finely sliced pieces of fruit and fruit peel distributed throughout the mixture. Marmalades are generally made from citrus fruits.

Preserves differ from jams in that the fruits are not crushed, but left whole and cooked in a syrup until the liquid mixture reaches the jelly stage.

Essentials for Good Jellied Products

Fruit, pectin, acid, and sugar are essential in making good jellied fruit products. Fruit is the single ingredient that gives all jellied products their characteristic flavor. It also supplies a part of the acid and pectin necessary to make the mixture jell.

Pectin is a natural thickening agent present in all fruits; its amount varies in different fruits as well as in different varieties of the same fruit. All fruits have more pectin when they are ripe than when they are underripe or overripe. Fruits generally low in pectin (peaches and raspberries) should have commercial pectin, made from citrus fruit or apples, added to them. Many homemakers prefer using commercial pectin because the cooking time is shorter and more precise and the yield is much higher. In making jellies with commercial pectin, be sure to follow the directions on the package, since there is a difference in method when using the powdered or liquid pectin.

Acid, also present to some degree in all fruits, is needed for flavor and gel formation. As with pectin, the acid content varies with the kind of fruit and its stage of maturity. Underripe fruit usually has a higher acid content than fully ripe fruit. As a general rule, some underripe fruit should be used in combination with fully ripened fruit for superior flavor, color, and consistency. Commercial pectin contains some acid; for the low-acid fruits (raspberries and peaches), lemon juice is suggested as an ingredient to supply additional acid for satisfactory gel formation.

Sugar has a firming effect on the fruit, helps in gel formation, serves as a preserving agent, and adds to the flavor of the jellied product. Beet and cane sugar can be used with equal success. Half of the sugar called for in the recipe can be replaced with corn syrup or honey.

General Instructions for Jellied Products

Equipment: A large flat-bottomed kettle is essential in making jellied products. An 8- to 10-quart kettle is a good size.

A jelly or candy thermometer is helpful when making jellied products without the use of commercial pectin. Cooking the product to 220° or 221° will yield the desired consistency.

A jelly bag or a fruit press extracts juice for jelly-making purposes. The bag can be made of several thicknesses of cheesecloth or of flannel with the napped side in. A special stand or colander helps hold the jelly bag while the juice is being extracted.

Containers: Jelly glasses or canning jars may be used. Be sure all jars and closures are in perfect condition. Use new lids for jars.

Have the glasses or jars ready before beginning any actual jelly or jam production. Wash the jars in warm suds, rinse in hot water, boil 10 minutes to sterilize, and keep hot until used. This prevents cracking when filled.

Wash and rinse all lids and bands. Metal lids with sealing compound may require immersion in hot water for a short time before using; follow the manufacturer's directions for this. When using porcelain-lined zinc caps, have new rings of the right size for jars. Caps may be reused, but new rings should be used. Wash the rings in hot soapy water, and rinse well.

Packing and Sealing: Prepare jars and lids ahead so they will be ready to fill.

To seal with lids, use only standard home canning jars and lids. For jars with metal lids and bands, fill the hot jars to within 1/8 inch of the top with the hot fruit mixture. Wipe the jar rim clean and place a hot metal lid on the jar with sealing compound next to the glass; screw the metal lid down firmly and stand the jar upright to cool. For jars with porcelain-lined zinc caps, place a wet rubber ring on the shoulder of an empty jar. Fill the jar to within 1/8 inch of the top, screw the cap down tightly, and stand jar upright to cool. When using either type lid, work quickly. After the jar has been filled, use a knife to remove air bubbles by moving the blade around the jar edges.

In many instances, it is wise to process jams, conserves, marmalades, and preserves for 10 minutes in a boiling-water bath after sealing with lids. If your recipe does not call for processing, you may prefer to seal the jars with paraffin.

The method of sealing with paraffin should be used only with mixtures that make fairly firm products. Use only enough paraffin to make a layer 1/8 inch thick, and prick air bubbles in the paraffin before it gets firm. Do not use paraffin that has been used before. Never melt paraffin over direct heat; use a double boiler.

For jelly, pour the hot juice mixture immediately into the hot glass containers to within 1/2 inch of top, and cover with hot paraffin. For jam, conserves, preserves, and marmalade, remove the fruit mixture from the heat; skim and stir about 5 minutes. This will help prevent the fruit from floating to the top. Before each stirring, skim off the foam. Pour the fruit mixture into hot glasses to within 1/2 inch of top. Remove air bubbles with a knife, and cover with a 1/8-inch layer of paraffin. Cover with lids.

Cooling and Storing: Let sealed jars stand overnight to be sure that the seal has been made. Label with name of jellied product and date; also include batch number if you make more than one batch. Store in a cool, dark, dry place. Do not hold jellied products in storage longer than one year. Uncooked jams may be stored in the refrigerator 3 weeks; if longer storage is needed, place them in the freezer.

BLACKBERRY JELLY

About 3 quarts ripe blackberries
7½ cups sugar
2 (3-ounce) packages liquid fruit
  pectin

Sort and wash berries; remove any stems or caps. Crush berries to extract 4 cups juice. Combine juice and sugar in a large saucepan and mix well. Place over high heat and stir until mixture comes to a hard boil. Boil hard 1 minute, stirring constantly. Add pectin and bring to a full rolling boil; boil 1 minute, stirring constantly. Remove from heat. Skim off foam with a metal spoon. Pour quickly into hot sterilized jars, leaving ½-inch headspace. Seal with a ⅛-inch layer of paraffin. Cover with lids. Yield: about 4 pints.

GRAPE JELLY

About 3½ pounds Concord grapes
½ cup water
7 cups sugar
1 (3-ounce) package liquid fruit
  pectin

Sort and wash grapes; remove stems. Crush grapes and add to water in a Dutch oven, mixing well. Cover and place over high heat until mixture comes to a boil. Reduce heat and simmer 10 minutes. Press mixture through a cheesecloth or strainer, extracting 4 cups juice.

Allow juice to sit overnight in a cool place. Strain juice through a double thickness of damp cheesecloth.

Combine juice and sugar in a large Dutch oven, stirring well. Place over high heat; cook, stirring constantly, until mixture comes to a rapid boil. Add pectin, and bring to a full rolling boil; boil 1 minute, stirring constantly.

Remove from heat, and skim off foam with a metal spoon. Pour quickly into hot sterilized jars, leaving ½-inch headspace; seal with a ⅛-inch layer of paraffin. Cover with lids. Yield: about 4 pints.
Virginia Outhouse,
Tavares, Fla.

MUSCADINE JAM

2 quarts muscadines
6 cups sugar

Remove stems and skins from muscadines. Cook pulp over low heat until soft; press through a sieve or food mill to remove seeds. Combine pulp and sugar in a large saucepan; cook over medium heat, stirring occasionally, until mixture comes to a boil. Boil almost to jellying point (220°), about 10 minutes, stirring frequently.

Remove from heat and skim off foam with a metal spoon. Ladle quickly into hot sterilized jars, leaving ¼-inch headspace. Cover at once with metal lids, and screw bands tight. Process in boiling-water bath for 15 minutes. Yield: about 3 pints.

Note: Muscadine skins may be added to jam. Chop skins in a food processor. Combine skins and about ½ cup water in a saucepan; simmer 15 to 20 minutes. Add to pulp and sugar and proceed as above.

FREEZER STRAWBERRY JAM

3 cups fresh strawberries
5 cups sugar
1 (1¾-ounce) package powdered fruit pectin
1 cup water

Remove stems from strawberries; rinse and drain. Puree strawberries in container of electric blender; combine puree and sugar, stirring well. Set aside 10 minutes.

Stir pectin into water. Bring to a boil; boil 1 minute. Pour pectin mixture into puree; stir 3 minutes. Ladle into sterilized freezer jars, sealing at once with metal lids, or ladle into frozen food containers and seal at once with plastic lids. Allow to stand at room temperature for 24 hours. Store in freezer. Yield: about 3 pints.

Note: Jam may also be used as ice cream topping. Let stand at room temperature 10 to 15 minutes before serving. *Mrs. Galen Johnson,*
Transylvania, La.

FIG PRESERVES

4 quarts fresh figs with stems
1 tablespoon soda
3 quarts boiling water
8 cups sugar
1 quart water
1 lemon, thinly sliced

Place figs in a large bowl; sprinkle with soda. Add 3 quarts boiling water, and soak 1 hour. Drain figs; rinse thoroughly in cold water.

Combine sugar and 1 quart water in a large Dutch oven; bring to a boil, and cook 10 minutes. Add figs and lemon to syrup; cook until figs are clear and tender (about 1 hour), stirring occasionally.

Spoon figs into hot sterilized jars; if necessary, continue cooking syrup until thick. Pour syrup over figs, leaving ¼-inch headspace. Run knife around edge of jars to remove air bubbles. Cover at once with metal lids, and screw bands tight. Process in boiling-water bath for 10 minutes. Yield: 4 to 5 pints.

Note: Any remaining syrup can be poured into a hot sterilized jar, sealed, processed, and used as a topping for pancakes or ice cream.

PEACH PRESERVES

3½ cups sugar
2 cups water
5 cups sliced peaches (about 5 large)

Combine sugar and water in a large Dutch oven; cook over medium heat, stirring constantly, until sugar dissolves. Add peaches; bring to a boil and cook 20 minutes or until peaches are clear, stirring occasionally. Remove from heat; cover and let stand 12 to 18 hours in a cool place.

Drain peaches, reserving liquid in pan. Spoon peaches into hot sterilized jars; set aside. Bring liquid to a boil and cook 2 to 3 minutes, stirring often. Pour over peaches, leaving ¼-inch headspace. Cover at once with metal lids, and screw bands tight. Process in boiling-water bath for 15 minutes. Yield: about 2½ pints.

PLUM CONSERVE

2½ quarts (about 4 pounds) pitted, chopped plums
¾ cup thinly sliced orange rind
1¾ cups chopped orange pulp (about 2 large oranges)
2 cups raisins
6 cups sugar
2 cups broken pecans

Combine plums, orange rind and pulp, raisins, and sugar in a large saucepan. Cook over medium heat, stirring occasionally, until mixture comes to a boil. Boil until mixture almost reaches jellying point (220°), about 10 to 15 minutes, stirring frequently. Stir in pecans and cook 5 minutes, stirring frequently. Ladle quickly into sterilized jars, leaving ¼-inch headspace. Cover at once with metal lids, and screw bands tight. Process in boiling-water bath for 15 minutes. Yield: about 5 pints.

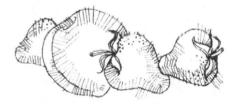

STRAWBERRY-PINEAPPLE MARMALADE

2½ cups finely chopped (about 1 medium) fresh pineapple
1 teaspoon grated orange rind
2½ cups chopped orange pulp (about 4 medium oranges)
7 cups sugar
1½ quarts strawberries

Combine pineapple, orange rind and pulp, and sugar in a large saucepan. Cook over medium heat, stirring occasionally, until mixture boils and sugar dissolves; boil 15 minutes. Add strawberries and boil until thick, about 20 to 30 minutes, stirring frequently. Pour quickly into sterilized jars. Cover at once with metal lids, and screw bands tight. Process jars in boiling-water bath for 10 minutes. Yield: about 3 pints.

Appendices

EQUIVALENT WEIGHTS AND MEASURES

Food	Weight or Count	Measure or Yield
Apples	1 pound (3 medium)	3 cups sliced
Bacon	8 slices cooked	½ cup crumbled
Bananas	1 pound (3 medium)	2½ cups sliced, or about 2 cups mashed
Bread	1 pound	12 to 16 slices
	About 1½ slices	1 cup soft crumbs
Butter or margarine	1 pound	2 cups
	¼ - pound stick	½ cup
Cabbage	1 pound head	4½ cups shredded
Candied fruit or peels	½ pound	1¼ cups cut
Carrots	1 pound	3 cups shredded
Cheese, American or Cheddar	1 pound	About 4 cups shredded
cottage	1 pound	2 cups
cream	3 - ounce package	6 tablespoons
Chocolate morsels	6 - ounce package	1 cup
Cocoa	1 pound	4 cups
Coconut, flaked or shredded	1 pound	5 cups
Coffee	1 pound	80 tablespoons (40 cups perked)
Corn	2 medium ears	1 cup kernels
Cornmeal	1 pound	3 cups
Crab, in shell	1 pound	¾ to 1 cup flaked
Crackers		
chocolate wafers	19 wafers	1 cup crumbs
graham crackers	14 squares	1 cup fine crumbs
saltine crackers	28 crackers	1 cup finely crushed
vanilla wafers	22 wafers	1 cup finely crushed
Cream, whipping	1 cup (½ pint)	2 cups whipped
Dates, pitted	1 pound	3 cups chopped
	8 - ounce package	1½ cups chopped
Eggs	5 large	1 cup
whites	8 to 11	1 cup
yolks	12 to 14	1 cup
Flour		
all-purpose	1 pound	3½ cups
cake	1 pound	4¾ to 5 cups sifted
whole wheat	1 pound	3½ cups unsifted
Green pepper	1 large	1 cup diced
Lemon	1 medium	2 to 3 tablespoons juice; 2 teaspoons grated rind
Lettuce	1 pound head	6¼ cups torn
Lime	1 medium	1½ to 2 tablespoons juice
Macaroni	4 ounces (1 cup)	2¼ cups cooked
Marshmallows	11 large	1 cup
	10 miniature	1 large marshmallow
Marshmallows, miniature	½ pound	4½ cups
Milk		
evaporated	5.33 - ounce can	⅔ cup
evaporated	13 - ounce can	1⅝ cups
sweetened condensed	14 - ounce can	1¼ cups
Mushrooms	3 cups raw (8 ounces)	1 cup sliced cooked

EQUIVALENT WEIGHTS AND MEASURES (*continued*)

Food	Weight or Count	Measure or Yield
Nuts		
almonds	1 pound	1 to 1¾ cups nutmeats
	1 pound shelled	3½ cups nutmeats
peanuts	1 pound	2¼ cups nutmeats
	1 pound shelled	3 cups
pecans	1 pound	2¼ cups nutmeats
	1 pound shelled	4 cups
walnuts	1 pound	1⅔ cups nutmeats
	1 pound shelled	4 cups
Oats, quick-cooking	1 cup	1¾ cups cooked
Onion	1 medium	½ cup chopped
Orange	1 medium	⅓ cup juice; 2 tablespoons grated rind
Peaches	4 medium	2 cups sliced
Pears	4 medium	2 cups sliced
Potatoes, white	3 medium	2 cups cubed cooked or 1¾ cups mashed
sweet	3 medium	3 cups sliced
Raisins, seedless	1 pound	3 cups
Rice, long-grain	1 cup	3 to 4 cups cooked
pre-cooked	1 cup	2 cups cooked
Shrimp, raw in shell	1½ pounds	2 cups (¾ pound) cleaned, cooked
Spaghetti	7 ounces	About 4 cups cooked
Strawberries	1 quart	4 cups sliced
Sugar		
brown	1 pound	2¼ cups firmly packed
powdered	1 pound	3½ cups unsifted
granulated	1 pound	2 cups

EQUIVALENT MEASUREMENTS

Use standard measuring cups (both dry and liquid measure) and measuring spoons when measuring ingredients. All measurements given below are level.

3 teaspoons	1 tablespoon
4 tablespoons	¼ cup
5⅓ tablespoons	⅓ cup
8 tablespoons	½ cup
16 tablespoons	1 cup
2 tablespoons (liquid)	1 ounce
1 cup	8 fluid ounces
2 cups	1 pint (16 fluid ounces)
4 cups	1 quart
4 quarts	1 gallon
⅛ cup	2 tablespoons
⅓ cup	5 tablespoons plus 1 teaspoon
⅔ cup	10 tablespoons plus 2 teaspoons
¾ cup	12 tablespoons
Few grains (or dash)	Less than ⅛ teaspoon
Pinch	As much as can be taken between tip of finger and thumb

HANDY SUBSTITUTIONS

Even the best of cooks occasionally runs out of an ingredient she needs and is unable to stop what she is doing to go to the store. At times like those, sometimes another ingredient or combination of ingredients can be used. Here is a list of substitutions and equivalents that yield satisfactory results in most cases.

Ingredient Called For	Substitution
1 cup self-rising flour	1 cup all-purpose flour plus 1 teaspoon baking powder and ½ teaspoon salt
1 cup cake flour	1 cup sifted all-purpose flour minus 2 tablespoons
1 cup all-purpose flour	1 cup cake flour plus 2 tablespoons
1 teaspoon baking powder	½ teaspoon cream of tartar plus ¼ teaspoon soda
1 tablespoon cornstarch or arrowroot	2 tablespoons all-purpose flour
1 tablespoon tapioca	1½ tablespoons all-purpose flour
2 large eggs	3 small eggs
1 egg	2 egg yolks (for custard)
1 egg	2 egg yolks plus 1 tablespoon water (for cookies)
1 cup commercial sour cream	1 tablespoon lemon juice plus evaporated milk to equal 1 cup; or 3 tablespoons butter plus ⅞ cup sour milk
1 cup yogurt	1 cup buttermilk or sour milk
1 cup sour milk or buttermilk	1 tablespoon vinegar or lemon juice plus sweet milk to equal 1 cup
1 cup fresh milk	½ cup evaporated milk plus ½ cup water
1 cup fresh milk	3 to 5 tablespoons nonfat dry milk solids in 1 cup water
1 cup honey	1¼ cups sugar plus ¼ cup liquid
1 (1-ounce) square unsweetened chocolate	3 tablespoons cocoa plus 1 tablespoon butter or margarine
1 clove fresh garlic	1 teaspoon garlic salt or ⅛ teaspoon garlic powder
1 teaspoon onion powder	2 teaspoons minced onion
1 tablespoon fresh herbs	1 teaspoon dried herbs or ¼ teaspoon powdered herbs
¼ cup chopped fresh parsley	1 tablespoon dehydrated parsley
1 teaspoon dry mustard	1 tablespoon prepared mustard
1 pound fresh mushrooms	6 ounces canned mushrooms

METRIC MEASURE/CONVERSION CHART

When You Know . . .	Approximate Conversion to Metric Measures		
	Multiply by . . .	To Find . . .	Symbol
	Mass (weight)		
ounces	28	grams	g
pounds	0.45	kilograms	kg
	Volume		
teaspoons	5	milliliters	ml
tablespoons	15	milliliters	ml
fluid ounces	30	milliliters	ml
cups	0.24	liters	l
pints	0.47	liters	l
quarts	0.95	liters	l
gallons	3.8	liters	l

Fahrenheit to Celsius: Subtract 32 • Multiply by 5 • Divide by 9
Celsius to Fahrenheit: Multiply by 9 • Divide by 5 • Add 32

CANNED FOOD GUIDE

Can Size	Number of Cups	Number of Servings	Foods
8-ounce	1 cup	2 servings	Fruits, Vegetables
10½- to 12-ounce (picnic)	1¼ cups	3 servings	Condensed Soups, Fruits and Vegetables, Meats and Fish, Specialties
12-ounce (vacuum)	1½ cups	3 to 4 servings	Vacuum-Packed Corn
14- to 16-ounce (No. 300)	1¾ cups	3 to 4 servings	Pork and Beans, Meat Products, Cranberry Sauce
16- to 17-ounce (No. 303)	2 cups	4 servings	Principal Size for Fruits and Vegetables, Some Meat Products
1 pound, 4 ounce (No. 2)	2½ cups	5 servings	Juices, Pineapple, Apple Slices
27- to 29-ounce (No. 2½)	3½ cups	7 servings	Fruits, Some Vegetables (Pumpkin, Sauerkraut, Greens, Tomatoes)
46-ounce (No. 3 cyl.)	5¾ cups	10 to 12 servings	Fruit and Vegetable Juices
6½-pound (No. 10)	12 to 13 cups	25 servings	Institutional Size for Fruits and Vegetables

VEGETABLE GUIDE

Selecting and Storing Vegetables

1. Buy fresh vegetables in season that are crisp, bright in color, and free from decay.

2. Compare prices of fresh versus frozen or canned vegetables. For example, if you are buying tomatoes for soup, you may find that canned ones would be the most economical. Some vegetables will remain fresh for a day or so after picking; others, like corn, start losing their flavor as soon as they are picked.

3. Buy only that amount of vegetables which can be stored properly. Although most vegetables should be washed and dried before storing, potatoes, onions, and garlic should never be washed. Do not soak fresh vegetables; too much moisture increases the possibility of spoilage and decay. Store immediately in vegetable crisper of refrigerator, or wrap in plastic wrap or plastic bags, and refrigerate. Immediate storage helps vegetables retain freshness and nutritional value. To prevent browning of leaves keep head lettuce intact without removing core or leaves until ready to use.

4. Put frozen vegetables into the freezer as soon as possible after purchase. Follow package directions about thawing before cooking. If frozen packages have been broken, rewrap in moistureproof paper or aluminum foil.

5. Store canned foods in a cool, dry place. Discard any cans that are puffed at ends—usually an indication of spoilage.

Amount to Buy	Servings per Pound or Unit	Amount to Buy	Servings per Pound or Unit
Artichokes	1	Green Pepper	½ to 1 whole per serving
Asparagus	3 or 4	Greens	4 or 5
Beans, snap or green	4	Mushrooms	4
Beets, diced, without tops	4	Okra	4
Broccoli	3 or 4	Onions, cooked	3 or 4
Brussels Sprouts	4 to 6	Peas	¾ pound per serving
Cabbage		Potatoes	2 or 3
Cooked	3 or 4	Rhubarb	4 or 5
Raw, diced or shredded	6 to 8	Rutabaga	2 or 3
Carrots		Spinach	
Cooked	3 or 4	Cooked	3
Raw, diced or shredded	5 or 6	Raw	6
Cauliflower	3 or 4	Squash, summer	3 or 4
Celery, raw	8 to 10	Squash, winter	2 or 3
Corn	1 to 2 ears per serving	Sweet Potatoes	3
Cucumber	1 regular for 2 to 3 servings	Tomatoes	4 or 5
Dry Beans, Peas, or Lentils	10 or 11	Turnip	4 or 5
Eggplant	4		

COOKING HINTS

Baking	Unless otherwise specified, always preheat the oven at least 20 minutes before baking.
Browning	For best results in browning food in a skillet, dry the food first on paper towels.
Measuring	Always measure accurately. Level dry ingredients with top of a cup or a knife edge or a spoon handle. Measure liquids in a cup so that the fluid is level with the top of the measuring line. Measure solid shortening by packing it firmly in a graduated measuring cup.
Storing	Milk cartons make splendid freezing containers for stocks, soups, etc. They also serve well for freezing fish or shrimp, foods that should be frozen in water.
Baking Powder	Always use double-acting baking powder.
Breads and Cakes	To test for doneness in baking a butter or margarine cake, insert a straw or wire cake tester into the center of the cake in at least two places. The tester should come out clean if the cake is done. The cake should be lightly browned and should be beginning to shrink from the pan's sides. If the cake is pressed with a finger in the center, it should come back into shape at once. If cake tests done, remove from oven, invert cakepan for 5 minutes (or time specified in the instructions); then loosen the cake from the sides and bottom of the pan. Invert it onto a plate or cake rack and turn it right side up on another cake rack so that air may circulate around it. This prevents sogginess. A sponge cake should be tested for doneness in the same manner as a butter cake, but keep the sponge cake inverted until it is thoroughly cold. Then run a knife around the sides and across the bottom and remove from pan. Trim off any hard edges. To test bread made with fruit or nuts, thump the crust and if it sounds hollow, remove the bread from the oven and cool on a wire rack. Bread cooked with fruit or nuts should be tested with a straw in the center. The straw should come out perfectly clean if the bread is done.
Butter	When a recipe says "greased pan," grease the pan with solid shortening or an oil, unless butter is specified. Do not use whipped margarine in place of butter unless the recipe calls for melting the butter.
Candies	The weather is a big factor in candymaking. On a hot, humid day it is advisable to cook candy 2° higher than in cold, dry weather.
Eggs	Unused or extra egg whites may be frozen and used as needed. Make meringues or angel pies with the whites later. Egg whites freeze well and do not need to be defrosted. When boiling eggs, add 1 teaspoon salt to the water. This prevents a cracked egg from draining into the water.
Fruit	A whole lemon heated in hot water for 5 minutes will yield 1 or 2 tablespoons more juice than an unheated lemon.
Sauces	When a sauce curdles, remove pan from heat and plunge into a pan of cold water to stop cooking process. Beat sauce vigorously or pour into a blender and beat. When making a cream or white sauce, melt butter, add flour, and blend well. Remove from heat before adding warmed milk. It should never lump.
Seafood	For improved texture and flavor with canned shrimp, soak shrimp for 1 hour in ice water; drain. One pound raw shrimp yields about 2 cups cooked and peeled shrimp.
Vegetables	Cooking such vegetables as green peppers and cucumbers briefly in boiling water makes them more digestible than raw vegetables. All strings can be easily removed from string beans after washing if they are plunged into boiling water for 5 minutes. Drain in colander and string. New potatoes should be cooked in boiling water. Old potatoes should start in cold water and be brought to a boil. When vegetables or other foods scorch in cooking, immediately remove the pan's cover and the contents and plunge the saucepan into cold water for 20 to 30 minutes. Wash saucepan and return contents and resume cooking. Rub hands with parsley to remove any odor.

GLOSSARY

à la King—Food prepared in a creamy white sauce containing mushrooms and red and/or green peppers

à la Mode—Food served with ice cream

al Dente—The point in the cooking of pasta at which it is still fairly firm to the tooth; that is, very slightly undercooked

Aspic—A jellied meat juice or a liquid held together with gelatin

au Gratin—Food served crusted with breadcrumbs or shredded cheese

au Jus—Meat served in its own juice

Bake—To cook food in an oven by dry heat

Barbecue—To roast meat slowly over coals on a spit or framework, or in an oven, basting intermittently with a special sauce

Baste—To spoon pan liquid over meats while they are roasting to prevent surface from drying

Beat—To mix vigorously with a brisk motion with spoon, fork, egg beater, or electric mixer

Béchamel—White sauce made of butter, flour, cream (not milk), and seasonings

Bisque—A thick, creamy soup usually of shellfish, but sometimes made of pureed vegetables

Blanch—To dip briefly into boiling water

Blend—To stir 2 or more ingredients together until well mixed

Blintz—A cooked crêpe stuffed with cheese or other filling

Boil—To cook food in boiling water or liquid that is mostly water (at 212°) in which bubbles constantly rise to the surface and burst

Boiling-water-bath canning method—Used for processing acid foods, such as fruits, tomatoes, pickled vegetables, and sauerkraut. These acid foods are canned safely at boiling temperatures in a water-bath canner.

Borscht—Soup containing beets and other vegetables, usually with a meat stock base

Bouillabaisse—A highly seasoned fish soup or chowder containing two or more kinds of fish

Bouillon—Clear soup made by boiling meat in water

Bouquet Garni—Herbs tied in cheesecloth which are cooked in a mixture and removed before serving

Bourguignon—Name applied to dishes containing Burgundy and often braised onions and mushrooms

Braise—To cook slowly with liquid or steam in a covered utensil. Less-tender cuts of meat may be browned slowly on all sides in a small amount of shortening, seasoned, and water added.

Bread, to—To coat with crumbs, usually in combination with egg or other binder

Broil—To cook by a direct source of heat, either under the heat of a broiler, over hot coals, or between two hot surfaces

Broth—A thin soup, or a liquid in which meat, fish, or vegetables have been boiled

Capers—Buds from a Mediterranean plant, usually packed in brine and used as a condiment in dressings or sauces

Caramelize—To cook white sugar in a skillet over medium heat, stirring constantly, until sugar forms a golden-brown syrup

Casserole—An ovenproof baking dish, usually with a cover; also the food cooked in it

Charlotte—A molded dessert containing gelatin, usually formed in a glass dish or a pan that is lined with ladyfingers or pieces of cake

Chop—A cut of meat usually attached to a rib

Chop, to—To cut into pieces, with a sharp knife or kitchen shears

Clarified butter—Butter that has been melted and chilled. The solid is then lifted away from the liquid and discarded. Clarification heightens the smoke point of butter. Clarified butter will stay fresh in the refrigerator for at least 2 months.

Coat—To cover completely, as in "coat with flour"

Cocktail—An appetizer; either a beverage or a light, highly seasoned food, served before a meal

Compote—Mixed fruit, raw or cooked, usually served in "compote" dishes

Condiments—Seasonings that enhance the flavor of foods with which they are served

Consommé—Clear broth made from meat

Cool—To let food stand at room temperature until not warm to the touch

Court Bouillon—A highly seasoned broth made with water and meat, fish or vegetables, and seasonings

Cream, to—To blend together, as sugar and butter, until mixture takes on a smooth, cream-like texture

Cream, whipped—Cream that has been whipped until it is stiff

Crème de Cacao—A chocolate-flavored liqueur

Crème de Café—A coffee-flavored liqueur

Crêpes—Very thin pancakes

Croquette—Minced food, shaped like a ball, patty, cone, or log, bound with a heavy sauce, breaded and fried

Croutons—Cubes of bread, toasted or fried, served with soups, salads, or other foods

Cruller—A doughnut of twisted shape, very light in texture

Cube, to—To cut into cube-shaped pieces

Curacao—Orange-flavored liqueur

Cut in, to—To incorporate by cutting or chopping motions, as in cutting shortening into flour for pastry

Demitasse—A small cup of coffee served after dinner

Devil, to—To prepare with hot seasoning or sauce

Dice—To cut into small cubes

Dissolve—To mix a dry substance with liquid until the dry substance becomes a part of the solution

Dot—To scatter small bits of butter over top of a food

Dredge—To coat with something, usually flour or sugar

Filé—Powder made of sassafras leaves used to season and thicken foods

Fillet—Boneless piece of meat or fish

Flambé—To flame, as in Crêpes Suzette or in some meat cookery, using alcohol as the burning agent; flame causes caramelization, enhancing flavor

Flan—In France, a filled pastry; in Spain, a custard

Florentine—A food containing, or placed upon, spinach

Flour, to—To coat with flour

Fold—To add a whipped ingredient, such as cream or egg white to another ingredient by gentle over and under movement

Frappé—A drink whipped with ice to make a thick, frosty consistency

Fricassee—A stew, usually of poultry or veal

Fritter—Vegetable or fruit dipped into, or combined with, batter and fried

Fry—To cook in hot shortening

Garnish—A decoration for a food or drink

Glaze (To make a shiny surface)—In meat preparation, a jelled broth applied to meat surface; in breads and pastries, a wash of egg or syrup; for doughnuts and cakes, a sugar preparation coating

Grill—To broil under or over a source of direct heat

Grits—Coarsely ground dried corn, served boiled, or boiled and then fried

Gumbo—Soup or stew made with okra

Herb—Aromatic plant used for seasoning and garnishing foods

Hollandaise—A sauce made of butter, egg, and lemon juice or vinegar

Hominy—Whole corn grains from which hull and germ are removed

Jardiniere—Vegetables in a savory sauce or soup

Julienne—Vegetables cut into long thin strips or a soup containing such vegetables

Kahlúa—A coffee-flavored liqueur

Kirsch—A cherry-flavored liqueur

Knead—To work a food (usually dough) by hand, using a folding-back and pressing-forward motion

Marinate, to—To soak food in a seasoned liquid

Meringue—A whole family of egg white-sugar preparations including pie topping, poached meringue used to top custard, crisp meringue dessert shells, and divinity candy

Mince—To chop into very fine pieces

Mornay—White sauce with egg, cream, and cheese added

Mousse—A molded dish based on meat or sweet whipped cream stiffened with egg white and/or gelatin (if mousse contains ice cream, it is called bombe)

Panbroil—To cook over direct heat in an uncovered skillet containing little or no shortening

Panfry—To cook in an uncovered skillet in small amount of shortening

Parboil—To partially cook in boiling water before final cooking

Pasta—A large family of flour paste products, such as spaghetti, macaroni, and noodles

Pâté (French for paste)—A paste made of liver or meat

Petit Four—A small cake, which has been frosted and decorated

Pilau or pilaf—A dish of the Middle East consisting of rice and meat or vegetables in a seasoned stock

Poach—To cook in liquid held below the boiling point

Pot Liquor—The liquid in which vegetables have been boiled

Preheat—To turn on oven so that desired temperature will be reached before food is inserted for baking

Puree—A thick sauce or paste made by forcing cooked food through a sieve

Reduce—To boil down, evaporating liquid from a cooked dish

Remoulade—A rich mayonnaise-based sauce containing anchovy paste, capers, herbs, and mustard

Render—To melt fat away from surrounding meat

Rind—Outer shell or peel of melon or fruit

Roast, to—To cook in oven by dry heat (usually applied to meats)

Roux—A mixture of butter and flour used to thicken gravies and sauces; it may be white or brown, if mixture is browned before liquid is added

Sauté—To fry food lightly over fairly high heat in a small amount of fat in a shallow, open pan

Scald—(1) To heat milk just below the boiling point (2) To dip certain foods into boiling water before freezing them (also called blanching)

Scallop—A bivalve mollusk of which only the muscle hinge is eaten; also to bake a food in a sauce topped with crumbs

Score—To cut shallow gashes on surface of food, as in scoring fat on ham before glazing

Sear—To brown surface of meat over high heat to seal in juices

Set—Term used to describe the consistency of gelatin when it has jelled enough to unmold

Shred—Break into thread-like or stringy pieces, usually by rubbing over the surface of a vegetable shredder

Simmer—To cook gently at a temperature below boiling point

Singe—To touch lightly with flame

Skewer—To fasten with wooden or metal pins or skewers

Soak—To immerse in water for a period of time

Soufflé—A spongy hot dish, made from a sweet or savory mixture (often milk or cheese), lightened by stiffly beaten egg whites

Steam—To cook food with steam either in a pressure cooker, on a platform in a covered pan, or in a special steamer

Steam-pressure canning method—Used for processing low-acid foods, such as meats, fish, poultry, and most vegetables. A temperature higher than boiling is required to can these foods safely. The food is processed in a steam-pressure canner at 10 pounds' pressure (240°) to ensure that all spoilage micro-organisms are destroyed.

Steep—To let food stand in not quite boiling water until the flavor is extracted

Stew—A mixture of meat or fish and vegetables cooked by simmering in its own juices and liquid, such as water and/or wine

Stir-fry—To cook quickly in oil over high heat, using light tossing and stirring motions to preserve shape of food

Stock—The broth in which meat, poultry, fish, or vegetables has been cooked

Syrupy—Thickened to about the consistency of egg white

Toast, to—To brown by direct heat, as in a toaster or under broiler

Torte—A round cake, sometimes made with breadcrumbs instead of flour

Tortilla—A Mexican flat bread made of corn or wheat flour

Toss—To mix together with light tossing motions, in order not to bruise delicate food, such as salad greens

Triple Sec—An orange-flavored liqueur

Veal—Flesh of a milk-fed calf up to 14 weeks of age

Velouté—White sauce made of flour, butter, and a chicken or veal stock, instead of milk

Vinaigrette—A cold sauce of oil and vinegar flavored with parsley, finely chopped onions and other seasonings; served with cold meats or vegetables

Whip—To beat rapidly to increase air and increase volume

Wok—A round bowl-shaped metal cooking utensil of Chinese origin used for stir-frying and steaming (with rack inserted) of foods

Index

COUNTRY LIVING RECIPES

Progressive Farmer:

Foods Editor: Jean Wickstrom Liles
Associate Foods Editor: Margaret Chason
Assistant Foods Editor: Susan McIntosh
Test Kitchens Director: Lynn Lloyd
Test Kitchens Staff: Martha Hinrichs, Diane Hogan,
    Laura Nestelroad, Karen Parker, Peggy Smith
Editorial Assistant: Catherine Barber
Photo Stylist: Beverly Morrow
Photographer: Charles Walton

Oxmoor House, Inc.:

Editor: Ann H. Harvey
Assistant Editor: Annette Thompson
Production Manager: Jerry Higdon

Designer: Faith Nance
Illustrator: Diana B. Smith

Notes

THE Magazine For You
if You Share Our Interest
in the South.

SOUTHERN LIVING
features articles to help make
life for you and your
family more comfortable,
more stimulating, more fun...

SOUTHERN LIVING is about your home and how to make a more attractive, more convenient, more comfortable place to live. Each issue brings you dozens of decorating and remodeling ideas you can adapt to your own surroundings.

SOUTHERN LIVING is about gardening and landscaping and how to make the outside of your home just as attractive as the inside. In addition to gardening features, you'll find a monthly garden calendar pinpointing what to plant and when, plus a "Letters to our Garden Editor" section to answer your own particular questions.

SOUTHERN LIVING is about good food and entertaining, with recipes and menu ideas that are sure to delight your family and friends. You'll discover recipes with a Southern accent from some of the South's superlative cooks.

SOUTHERN LIVING is about travel and just plain fun. Every new issue offers an information-packed monthly calendar of special events and happenings throughout the South, plus features on the many facinating places of interest the South has to offer.

To find out how you can receive SOUTHERN LIVING every month, simply write to: SOUTHERN LIVING, P. O. Box C-119, Birmingham, AL 35283.